SPLASH!

The Ten Remarkable Traits to Build Momentum in Life and Leadership

By Steve Gutzler

TABLE OF CONTENTS

INTRODUCTION

I'm the type of person who can't wait to get up in the morning. I know that sounds odd to some. Most mornings, I'm looking forward to the day – happy, optimistic, and enthused. But things started to sink for me in 1995, which was a tough year.

On the outside, things looked pristine and polished – dare I say almost perfect. People saw no real obvious clues of the internal battles swirling inside my soul. I had a wonderful wife, three healthy and active children, a calling and career on the rise, and a beautiful home complete with the family dog and cat.

Despite all the good things, I was now facing a new challenge: I was unemployed.

I put on a good face and put up a good fight. But unfortunately, some of my past mechanisms to dodge or evade the truth were caving in. Mounting bills and a shrinking self-concept faced me daily. My once-confident strides slowly began to resemble a crawl. Whether I was clinically depressed or mildly depressed, the one thing I knew is that I felt alone and trapped.

My defining moment came to me in a whisper. I share more about it in chapter 1. If you don't believe in divine encounters, then this book may not be for you because that's what I believe that whisper was. And this whisperer has now become a shout inside my soul; it drives me daily. It's created a momentum. I'm driven – driven by a purpose and calling greater than myself.

<u>A Purpose to Make a Splash</u>

I need to give a brief disclaimer – I wouldn't want to give the slightest impression I've arrived. I'm still very much a work in progress. I get down from time to time. But I firmly believe that, if you read the stories on the following pages, you too may hear your own whisper – a whisper calling you to something greater, to build momentum in your life and leadership.

The purpose of this book is to encourage you to discover *your splash;* I discovered *my splash* soon after hearing that whisper.

I was driving out of our subdivision on one of those typical Seattle rainy days. As I got in my car, I mumbled, "Why couldn't my calling be in a warm climate?" I rounded the corner to experience my second revelation in just a matter of days.

Standing at a bus stop were what appeared to be a huddled group of kindergartners. It looked like they were mumbling, too, and sharing my dreary mood. There was one exception – the little boy in the bright yellow raincoat with shiny black boots. He was not mumbling; he looked like he was laughing, giggling, and making a splash. I slowed my car and stopped. I watched in wonder as this little guy hopped in a 360-degree circle, twirling and splashing in the puddles. It was as if he were looking to the heavens saying, "Bring it on, big guy ... let's have fun!"

God as my witness, watching that little boy inspired me to stop the **whining** and start the **winning** – *one splash at a time.*

This book's purpose is to help you discover your own splash and create new exciting momentum around the things in your life that really matter:

- A splash with family and friends – one that has meaning, intentional purpose and a lasting legacy.
- A splash in your personal leadership that leads to massive momentum in your personal influence, impact, and inspiration for others.

- A splash in everyday encounters – leading right where you are, touching one life at a time with goodness and love.

Little did I know that those two simple encounters would help me discover my splash ... one that led me to form my own company, Leadership Quest, a Seattle-based leadership development company.

It's hard to believe now that I've delivered more than 2,500 presentations to a "who's who" list of clients including Microsoft, Starbucks, Boeing, Cisco, Starwood Corporation, and dozens of small- and medium-sized companies.

I'm honored and humbled to personally coach several senior leaders, including a prestigious list of CEOs, presidents, and leading entrepreneurs. I reference that to encourage you ... do not underestimate the power of your splash.

Together, we are going to discover *10 traits to build momentum in life and leadership*. Each one is critical and builds on the next. I'll offer you some actionable coaching questions and quick steps to create momentum at the conclusion of each chapter.

I believe **now** is the time for you to transform puddles into some new momentum around your dreams and personal goals.

I hope that what you encounter in these pages will make a small contribution to your own significant splash!

Chapter 1: Calling

"Everyone has a wonderful and unique purpose; we are not here by mistake." - Steve Gutzler

I recently had the privilege of speaking at a large conference in downtown Seattle. This was a group of 600 business leaders, many of whom oversee large organizations. My topic was Emotional Intelligence for Personal Leadership, and my goal was to help them become more effective leaders by growing their emotional intelligence.

Right before I was introduced, the woman in charge of the entire conference leaned over and said, "You know, Steve, we brought you here to encourage and inspire these leaders. You'd be surprised at how many are in a bit of a funk ... discouraged. They need something from you today that offers real lasting change."

It was just the encouragement I needed to "go for it."

"Thank you for the gift of your time," I said as my opener. I shared that I recently re-read *Jack: Straight from the Gut* by legendary former GE CEO Jack Welch.

In it, I read the following six rules for successful leadership:

1. Control your destiny, or someone else will.
2. Face reality as it is, not as it was or as you wish it were.
3. Be candid with everyone.
4. Don't manage, lead.
5. Change before you have to.
6. If you don't have a competitive advantage, don't compete.

As I read this advice from the CEO of CEOs, I realized that five of the six rules for successful leadership were about facing reality – so I asked if I could respectfully toss some cold water on their face. They chuckled, but I could see their eyes open – more importantly, their hearts opened.

I shared that in order to lead well, you have to get real and honest with yourself – and face your own reality.

I then took a big risk and told a story of my defining moment of reality. It was 1995, and I was unemployed and in a major funk. I was depressed and despaired. On a walk in the back trails of our neighborhood, I was trying to think of any solutions and none were coming. Then it happened. I heard a soft whisper. It wasn't audible; it was more like an impression or penetrating thought. This is where the story gets a little risky.

I am pretty sure that the whisper came from God. He said to me, "Look up."

I did. I saw a huge fir tree – the kind we have everywhere in the Pacific Northwest. There were trees all around me, but this tree extended higher than the rest by far. The whisper said, "That tree is your life. I am going to do more than you can ask or imagine. We are not done; we are just getting started!"

I said to the audience, "Look, whether or not you believe in divine encounters, when I heard that whisper, I courageously faced my reality. And my reality didn't need a simple external makeover; it needed some lasting internal work."

For the first time in my life, I scribbled out a purpose statement – and have it to this day. Then I wrote five key values to guide my new purpose in the areas of *faith, family first, personal drive, leadership, and fun factor.*

I started writing new goals and activities around the <u>seven key areas of my life</u>: family, work/calling, health and fitness, personal development, finances, fun factor and spiritual peace.

I made a decision to dedicate myself to my new calling of inspiring greatness in others, and I followed through on a lifetime dream of taking other leaders on a leadership quest – the name of my company.

I shared with those leaders the truth I'd found: No one and no past experience can keep a person down who is dedicated to their true calling and purpose.

I then transitioned to my Emotional Intelligence topic. Following the keynote, I had several leaders thank me for including my story of the whisper. One man grabbed me by the hand and said, "You were my whisper today!"

In thinking through your calling, I would like to offer you a series of questions to create new momentum and perhaps revive a calling for the next era in your life and leadership.

1. What do you want the center of your life to be?
2. What is the character of your life – those handful of lasting values that guide you?
3. What is the communication of your life (your primary message and story)?
4. What will be your greatest contribution in life?

Determined like Diablo

I was finally going to take my own advice. For years I have been recommending recreation, as in *"re-create-tional"* activities to stay balanced and to recharge your emotional batteries and creative juices.

So here I was, ready to reinvigorate myself with horseback riding. I had been given a gift certificate for a 90-minute ride up into the foothills. I had been riding once or twice before and had fond memories of the experience; I especially enjoyed the pony rides in circles at the local fair when I was 5.

A cowgirl approached and simply asked, "Do you ride much? How good are you?" For whatever reason, I decided to lie. I basically told a big, bold-faced lie: "Well, I'm very good! Lots of riding experience in my background!" Really, I just didn't want to be stuck with one of those old, has-been grey horses that don't have any spark left in their eyes. I wanted a horse with some get-up; a horse that would trot and gallop!

They brought out a beautiful horse named Diablo. Diablo was a mare, but I don't think that word really summed her up. I'm not sure, but I think she was emotionally unstable. I know she lacked Emotional Intelligence! She was angry from the beginning. She was stubborn.

It took me 30 minutes to get her out of the barn and stable and up the trail. It was not a good match. The plan was to enjoy a relaxing ride up to the bluff and enjoy the meadow there ... *Ahhhh.* There would be a breeze and we could gallop across at a nice pace ... *Ahhhh.*

As you've probably guessed, the day did not go as planned. Instead, as soon as we got to the bluff, Diablo pulled a lightning-fast U-turn on me and started galloping for home. I pulled the reins but nothing happened; in fact, she went faster. I screamed. I said, *"Whhoooooaaaa!"* Nothing was working. She was hell-bent on getting back into that barn.

As we raced towards the barn at full speed, I had two choices – either bail off Diablo or duck low to get through the barn door. I decided to duck. She stopped immediately once she was inside and walked happily into her stall. I could almost hear her say "Ahhhhh, home."

The cowgirl came back, looking confused, and asked "Back already?" Trying to save face, I said "Yeah, I just wanted a quick little ride today. Thank you!" As I walked away from Diablo, I muttered to her, "You're nothing like Little Joe's horse ..."

I have to give Diablo some credit: She knew what she wanted!

1. What is your one thing that you want?
   You cannot market to the masses. You cannot shoot a bunch of shotgun pellets everywhere. You must focus on your ONE MAIN THING.
2. What is your primary goal?
   I'm going to suggest you narrow your focus in the next 90 days. (More on how to do that below!)
3. Get clear on your brand and your message.
   Find your strength and stay with it!
4. Become an expert in your field.
   Knowledge is power. Hone your craft.
5. Get single minded and determined.
   Not to say you can't enjoy variety, but you must know what you want and know your **one big goal.**

There will be days when people try to pull you in lots of directions away from your purpose and goal. Stay true and vigilant in your pursuit.

"Stick to your mission and say 'no' to things not mission-critical." - Steve Gutzler

If I could suggest one more thing to every leader I know, it would be to write down your **one big goal.** Then put 10 action items under that goal as to how you will make it happen!

Here are some closing thoughts that help me refocus when I am veering off from my one big goal:

1. Goals create positive energy and hope.
2. A clearly articulated goal offers you a North Star to guide you out of rough seas and into clear waters.
3. Know exactly what you want and clearly write it down.

"A person with a clear vision, personally and professionally, will make progress on a challenging road."
- Steve Gutzler

Questions to Build Momentum in: Calling

1.   What are five or six things or relationships you need to hang on to?

_____

_____

_____

2. What habit or hindrance do you need to let go of?

_____

_____

_____

3. What do you want to accomplish in the next two to three years?

_____

_____

_____

4. How would you hope people would describe you?

_____

_____

_____

5. Describe your calling/purpose, one that inspires you and influences others – your *splash!*

_____

_____

_____

Thoughts around Calling

As far back as I can remember, my mother would have me down by my bed at night with her, praying. I can still hear her voice calling my name to God and telling him that she wanted me to follow him in whatever he called me to do. – Charles R. Swindoll

The first time I walked on a stage, I knew that was what I was created to do. I know that there was a calling and a sense of purpose in my life that gave me fulfillment and a sense of destiny. – T.D. Jakes

The growth and development of people is the highest calling of leadership. – Harvey Firestone

It has been my observation that the happiest people, the vibrant doers of the world, are almost always those who are using – who are putting into play, calling upon, depending upon – the greatest number of their God-given talents and capacities. – John Glen

Calling is a process, and as life happens, there are tons of ups and downs – ebbs and flows. There are exciting mountaintops and heart-breaking valleys. In the end, if you don't quit, your true calling will emerge. – Steve Gutzler

If you're alive, there's a purpose for your life. – Rick Warren

Chapter 2: Code of Honor

"As you build your personal beliefs, you build your life." - Steve Gutzler

Flipping Pancakes

For nearly three-and-a-half decades, my parents owned and operated a restaurant called Tom's Pancake House. Not a burger joint, not a steakhouse, not one of those really posh places you go on your anniversary – just a little pancake house named after my father. He served up 30 different types of pancakes, some waffles, omelets, coffee, and hot chocolate ... yum! It was kind of a blue-collar restaurant. But white-collar people liked it, too, as we had some big names visit us – Nike co-founder Phil Knight lived just down the road and loved Tom's!

My father was born to own and operate that place. When you arrived, chances were that he would be up front with a big friendly smile to greet you. He only ever took Wednesdays off and loved working the busy weekend mornings; they were the bread-and-butter – or the "pancakes and syrup" – of the business.

My sister Becky and I cut our teeth on that restaurant business. I started working at the ripe age of 9 for two hours a week. (*Aren't there laws against that?*) Every Saturday, my mom would drop me off at 11 a.m. I worked my rigorous two-hour shift until 1 p.m. At noon, my dad would bring me an R.C. Cola. (*Remember those? Are they still around?*)

What was my job, you ask? Peeling potatoes!

Yep. Two hours of peeling potatoes a week. We served freshly cooked hash brown potatoes. None of that frozen, freeze-dried stuff for us – the old-fashioned, actual potato. I was too short to reach the counter so I would stand on an overturned milk crate. Steaming hot potatoes would be rolled out onto the counter for me to peel. I had a paper towel, a paring knife, and a bucket. Then I would place the potatoes on the drying rack. On a good day, we would cook five to six huge batches. It felt like mountains of potatoes to a 9-year-old; actually, it would probably feel like mountains to anyone!

If I was lucky, Candy, the prep woman, would help me. I look back and smile, thankful that my folks taught us the importance of good work ethic. I later moved up to dishwasher, busboy, host, and finally manager by 19.

At Tom's we had three business mantras:

1. **Meet and Greet the Customer:** If you walked into Tom's, you wouldn't have to worry about seating yourself or wonder where you are supposed to go. We had a 60 second rule: Get to the customer and meet-and-greet them with a smile within the first 60 seconds. For whatever reason, that is deeply ingrained in me. I still initiate the greetings in every business encounter. My father held an ironclad conviction for kindness, appreciation, and being cordial.

2. **Surprise and Delight:** In food service, this is very important! You must deliver what is expected, and then some! I have a sales team presentation based on this mantra called "The 'And Then Some' Attitude." In this multi-media, social media, high-tech, low-touch world, what would happen to your business if you gave yourself to "and then some?" What would happen if we surprised and delighted our clients and customers with more than they were expecting? Treat them like royalty and they will say those magic words: "I'll be back."

3. **Look Them in the Eyes and Say Thank You:** It only happened one time. I took money from a young family checking out. I thanked them, but failed to look them in the eyes. My father, ever

attentive, spotted me. After rush hour slowed, he took me aside and admonished me to "look them in the eyes." This was a second-generation customer I had been serving and I needed to treat each person that came in like royalty. He taught me that we need to appreciate each of our customers! Even as a 19-year-old kid, that lesson really sunk in.

Even now when I speak at leadership trainings to Fortune 500 companies, I still use these same three thoughts.

I slip occasionally – like we all do – but not often. My daughter was working on a major project in college several years ago and in it, included the fact that the number one lesson she learned from her parents was the value of appreciation. Look people in the eyes and tell them thank you.

Speaking of appreciation ... I want to make sure you know that I appreciate you, my readers! I appreciate you! You matter to me!

The Whitest of Whites

Here in Seattle, we regularly see iconic landmarks like the Space Needle, Pike Place Market, and, of course, boathouses like the one from *Sleepless in Seattle*.

We also have some pretty powerful corporate icons like Microsoft, Boeing, and Starbucks. I am proud and humbled to say each of those are valued clients of mine. I've trained teams and built extraordinary relationships with some spectacular leaders from those world-class companies.

If you are from the Seattle area, there is another name that might stand out to you – Gene Juarez Salons and Spas. It is the place for hair design, personal style, and the promotion of well-being.

Recently I was privileged to emcee at an amazing event where the founder of these salons was speaking – none other than Gene Juarez himself.

Gene came from humble beginnings. In 1971, he started his business with his imagination, his dreams, and a handful of rich values passed down from his parents and his culture.

I would like to focus on three points that stood out to me in his message and really made an impact on me. I was there scribbling down these points while he spoke and want to share them with you.

Imagine how values drive your success:

Value #1: Chop Wood and Carry Water - Work Ethic

Gene's parents taught him the value of personal drive. He said his parents would often tell him that no one works harder than the Juarezes! Gene said, "No matter how tough the economy is, if you outwork your competition, you can succeed."

Value #2: Whitest of Whites - Excellence

Like I mentioned, Gene's family came from modest means. His mother washed their clothes in a wash barrel, scrubbing each article by hand. She always washed and bleached the whites two times, even though it was twice as much work. It was a matter of pride and excellence to her to look your best. This is so clearly reflected in his salons and spas today – when you walk into a Gene Juarez location, it sparkles with excellence!

Value #3: Woman in the Mirror - Service

I love this one! Gene related to us at the event how, when cutting a woman's hair, he would ask her questions about how she wanted to look. He would study her eyes. Eyes, he said, are the gateway to the soul. She would either turn and speak to him in mild, timid ways, or she would look down and not feel pretty or confident. Sometimes, the woman would look confidently in the mirror and express her desires. The key, Gene said, was to study her eyes and her body language. His goal was to meet her individual needs, to make her feel beautiful. It was attention to their personal feelings about themselves that set his service apart. It made the experience personal and powerful. When they stepped out of that chair, away from the woman in the mirror, he wanted them to feel extraordinary about themselves.

"What you build today will either empower or restrict you tomorrow." - Steve Gutzler

HOW ABOUT YOU?

- On a scale of 1-10, how would you rate your **work ethic** as of late?

No matter what you do – whether you cut hair, sell insurance, lay tile, freelance write, own a small business, or work for a large corporation – work ethic is number one.

I coach all my clients to blueprint their week. Work hard on things that matter! Get away from what I call "fake work" – those trivial pursuits, those endless hours on Twitter and Facebook. Instead, get busy on your high-value accomplishments. You'll soon see greater results and profits!

- On a scale of 1-10, how would you rate your excellence?

It starts with appearance and moves to your craft. Look good and perform your best. It doesn't have to be perfect, but strive for excellence. *No one is inspired by low expectations, so expect the best from yourself!* Do excellent work, eat excellent food, read excellent books, spend time with excellent people. Make "excellence" your new mantra!

- On a scale of 1-10, how would you rate your service?

My dad operated a family restaurant for more than 30 years. He always told his employees and his children, "Treat everyone like a 10. There are no no-counts that come into our restaurant." Treat everyone like royalty. Do the extras, give them extra, and you will hear those magic words: "I'll be back!"

FINAL CHALLENGE:

As you head into a new business cycle, imagine and commit to a new level of supreme values personally and professionally. You will see greater results, rewards, and profits!

Who knows, some day you may become a city icon yourself!

Your code of honor allows you to make and keep promises to yourself.

– Steve Gutzler

Questions to Build Momentum in:
Code of Honor

1. What are eight to 10 promises you want to make and keep personally and professionally?

_____

_____

_____

2. Write a brief description for each promise listed above.

_____

_____

_____

3. Why do you think keeping promises is essential to making your splash?

_____

_____

_____

4. What is one promise you've broken that you can repair?

_____

_____

_____

*Remember: Greater awareness of your code creates better choices which lead to lasting results.

Thoughts Around Code of Honor

Your code of honor is eight to 10 promises you want to make and keep to yourself and others. – Steve Gutzler

Character cannot be developed in ease and quiet. Only through experience of trial and suffering can the soul be strengthened, ambition inspired, and success achieved. – Helen Keller

John Wooden was a hall of fame character long before he was a hall of fame coach. – John C. Maxwell

Code of honor is spelled I-N-T-E-G-R-I-T-Y. – Steve Gutzler

Beginning today, treat everyone you meet as if they were going to be dead by midnight. Extend to them all the care, kindness, and understanding you can master, and do it with no thought of any reward. Your life will never be the same again. – Og Mandino

Character may almost be called the highest and most effective means of persuasion. – Aristotle

It is better to be faithful than famous. – Theodore Roosevelt

The important things are children, honesty, integrity, and faith. – Andy Williams

Chapter 3: Vision

"The quickest way to advance your life is to reject old tapes that play in your mind. Play new tapes of a powerful future." – Steve Gutzler

The Pixie Kitchen

I live in the Seattle area now, but I grew up in Portland. As a young boy, my parents would take my sister and me on a couple hours' drive to the Oregon coast. One of our favorite destinations before hitting the beach was the Pixie Kitchen.

It was a unique restaurant with all sorts of colorful rooms and enchanting rides. My favorite room was the Room of Distortion. It was filled with mirrors that would change how you looked. Sometimes, you would be tall and sticklike or short and stocky. Sometimes, you were wavy. Sometimes, you looked smashed. We would all get the giggles and have a blast living in that world of make-believe.

Looking back now on the Room of Distortion, I think to myself …

What is your view of yourself?

I've come to realize through numerous coaching and training experiences that business executives, professional athletes, and even recognized celebrities all view themselves through a mirror. That includes you and me. We all have a funhouse-mirror image of ourselves, and that image of ourselves dictates a lot of our behavior and our performance levels.

Sometimes, our image is strong and confident while other times, it is weak and insecure. You might feel lovely and beautiful or ugly and unattractive.

Remember: That image is powerful and can dictate how we behave and how well we perform in daily activities and one-time experiences.

HOW TO LOOK AND LISTEN TO THE EXCEPTIONAL YOU:

Start with the Right Mirror Image

You'd be surprised at the number of high-profile clients who struggle with self-image, self-concept, and self-esteem.

Start by creating an image of yourself based on your own self-worth, not what an overbearing parent or highly critical boss used to tell you. It shouldn't be based on the number of hairs on your head or your body weight or the clothes in your closet. Instead, focus on what is good and right about you. Focus on the things that say how exceptionally smart and talented you are, on the things that depict how beautiful and handsome you are on the inside, on the things that show you that you are gifted and compassionate and created for success and positive contribution.

I coached a professional golfer who, at one time, was in the top 10 in the world. But over time, he got beat up by his defeats. Soon his image sunk and his game went down with it. We literally started from ground zero and rebuilt his self-image brick-by-brick by focusing on personal accomplishments.

If you looked at him now, you would have thought he was an attractive and confident athlete his whole life. But in reality, he was once very fragile and in need of some serious self-image repair.

How did we work together to turn his self-image around?

We made a list of six to eight personal affirmations. We looked at them each day and repeated these "Exceptional You" affirmations. We literally stood in the mirror and spoke the affirmations out loud to ourselves.

1. I am an exceptional person of high performance.
2. I am healthy and fit and attractive.
3. I am gifted and confident.
4. I am positive and magnetic with a personality that draws people to me.
5. I am caring and compassionate for others.
6. I am a thought leader and success achiever.
7. I am soulful and spiritually centered.

Your list should reflect you, your talents, and the areas where you are exceptional. We don't all have the same areas which is why we all need to work together and bring new things to the table. Maybe you don't have one of the same qualities as your older sibling, but there is no doubt that we all have something. You are exceptional.

Listen to the Right Tapes

Recently, I coached Karen, whose self-image plummeted over the years due to her father's destructive and cruel words. She struggled with her weight and with feeling unattractive. She had grown up in a home where she was compared to her younger sister who was "the pretty one."

She said, "Steve, every time I was to reach for success, I would hear my dad say 'you're fat' or 'why can't you be more like your younger sister?'"

To help her, we made Karen several index cards with new statements about who she was as a person. We removed the old, dated tape stuck on repeat in her mind and upgraded to a digital message of positivity, power, and purpose!

TRUE STORY: This then-single, quiet, and insecure young woman is now an executive at Microsoft, married with children and looks wonderful! She is radiant and confident.

Actions That Drive New Behaviors

Replace those old, negative thoughts with thoughts of the new, exceptional you! Then watch your behaviors slowly start to reflect those beliefs and uncover that new you. Be intentional about your messaging and be deliberate in correcting those negative thoughts that will creep in every once in a while. Listen and repeat the positive.

Your success is determined by your self-image, so align it to the Exceptional You!

Splash

Now is your time – your time to start living the life you had IMAGINED!

I was like a little kid standing in line at Disneyland – except this line led to something I had looked forward to seeing for years. I was standing in line in Florence, Italy, at the great art museum which housed my favorite Bible character – the statue of David. Julie and I had come to Italy to see all the majestic sites of that country, but this was the one I had been most looking forward to seeing.

As I rounded the corner, there stood David. Breathtaking. Unbelievable. Better, dare I say, than I had imagined!

I have often used the story of the creation of David's statue for years in my speaking. I am a storyteller, and this story is stuck deep in my heart and soul. The story of the creation of David is perfect for a series on imagination. Here's why:

Michelangelo was commissioned by the Medicis, one of the wealthiest and most powerful families in Italy, to create a statue for the main square in Florence. For two years, Michelangelo searched for the block of marble to create his masterpiece. Finally, on the back streets of Florence, covered by weeds and dirt, he found it.

He had walked past it many times, but this time he stopped, looked, and imagined his David in his mind's eye; he saw David in its entirety.

Then he arranged for his workmen to haul the slab to his studio. He went about the task of hammering and chiseling. It took him two years to create the basic outline of David.

It takes much time to create a masterpiece.

It was two more years of polishing and sanding before the statue was completed. *Six years total.* When it was unveiled, thousands came for the public viewing of Michelangelo's David. Now here I was, standing in line hundreds of years later to see the same statue. And I wasn't disappointed.

Afterward, when Michelangelo was asked how he was able to create such a masterpiece, he replied by saying:

He saw David complete and perfect in the marble. All he did was remove everything that was not David.

I have a big David-sized question for you: Have you taken time recently to imagine the masterpiece inside of you?

I know this sounds a bit grand, but I do believe each of our lives contains David-size possibilities. Our lives are contained in marble, if you will. Like a slab, we can seem a bit uninspiring until someone hauls us to the studio and starts hammering and chiseling. All we have to do is remove all the parts of ourselves that aren't David. Some of that process involves pain and some involves purpose, but all of it takes time.

There are so many things that can hold us back from realizing our "Imagined Life," like excessive fears, worries, doubts, and many more. Quite frankly, I think *the number one reason people fail to realize their masterpiece is that they want it quick and easy.*

I want to remind you it took Michelangelo six years to create David. And David was only made from marble, not from heart and soul and mind and spirit. *You are going to take much longer.* Be patient. You and I are created by a majestic God who has majestic plans for you. But it will take time.

Splash MOMENTS

Take time this week to really think about that masterpiece inside of you – your "Imagined Life." Formulate it in your mind's eye and then we'll talk about developing strategies for hammering and chiseling, sanding and polishing to make your David appear!

The Fog of Battle

They call it the fog of battle, where all you see and hear is gunfire. When you are in a battle, it is hard to maintain clear perspective. - Steve Gutzler

My phone was ringing. I looked down at it and read the caller ID and thought, "Wow, one of my favorite coaching clients!" I gave a cheerful hello only to hear a faint voice on the other end. You see, my friend was sitting in his car in a parking garage unable to get out. He was trapped in his car by his own fear and fatigue. This once-confident and self-assured president of a company was now childlike and meek.

He related to me over the phone how a series of downward disappointments had beat him up. He couldn't gather himself to "pull it together" and get out of the car to face another day of "battle."

I turned from coach to counselor. I tried my very best to encourage him to open the door and head back into it. I promised to meet with him soon for a day of VISIONEERING. Slowly, my friend's voice picked up volume and realization as he stated, "Steve, I've lost vision. All I see is the battle."

Vision is a picture of the future which creates passion in the present.

I drove to meet him at his location. We spent three hours together rebuilding, rediscovering, and renewing his vision.

Vision Question: How is your Vision? Not your sight; your Vision.

What do you see in your future?

Here is a simple but powerful place to start: "What is it that I really want to accomplish?"

This is your time to truly dream big. Don't focus on your current situation or the limitations you see around you. If it feels scary to dream this big, you may want to choose two or three areas to focus on and map out on a single sheet of paper. Do not get frozen or fearful. Give yourself permission to imagine the possibilities in your career! Maybe you want to focus on your health! Maybe you want to turn that blog into a book. Maybe you want to turn those daily bike rides into a successful bike race.

There are so many possibilities that you can accomplish in your life with the right type of Vision!

Remember what I just said about Michelangelo's creation process of David? Michelangelo stripped away everything that wasn't David. But first, he *Imagined* his *Vision* of David in his mind.

Ask yourself: What type of person do I want to be?

That question is a great place to begin developing your Vision. Perhaps you want to be more spiritual, healthier, more fit, more optimistic, or to have remarkable energy that is just irresistible! Here is one activity that can really help build and maintain the power of your vision:

BUILDING YOUR VISION BOARD

Lin is an award-winning interior designer, so she is a natural at creation. When I took Lin through the process of building her vision board, it turned out spectacular! It was aesthetically pleasing and organized. But not all boards have to be beautiful; they just have to display your vision in a way that you understand and that inspires you. On Lin's board, she placed a picture of her husband and herself boating in the San Juan Islands. She had a picture of herself working in her garden at home. She had inspiring phrases and quotes.

It was a colorful reminder of her vision of her future life. The idea of the Vision Board is to be a reminder of what we are striving to reach even when we are stuck in the fog of battle. It is a visual vacation that can pull us toward our future selves. Once you regain and maintain your personal and professional vision, energy and oxygen course into your soul and it will fuel your days!

Think about these things:
- What is that inspiring vision you have for the next two or three years?
- What do you really want to accomplish?
- What type of person would you be proud to be?
- If you were able to get out of the battle for three hours, what would your Vision Board look like?

NOTE:

I am pleased to report that my friend from the beginning of the chapter is better than ever. In fact, he recently sent me a wonderful spiritual book with a note that inspired me: "Steve, stay encouraged and stay spiritually whole. We need you." He just gave me some vision with that statement!

Imagine Your Vision Today!

"Great leaders act decisively in the absence of certainty." - Steve Gutzler

Questions to Build Momentum in: Vision

1. Michelangelo created David in his mind's eye.
    Can you take time to imagine in your mind's eye a
    vision filled with great accomplishments that will
    create an enduring splash?

    _____

    _____

    _____

2. What distorted image in your mind's eye has held
    you back from your true and authentic vision?

    _____

    _____

    _____

3. What powerful new personal affirmations can
    you record and state daily?

    _____

    _____

    _____

4. What two phrases need to be eliminated from
    your inner dialogue?

    _____

    _____

    _____

5. Create your vision board, a colorful graphic
    reminder of a future that will pull you forward.
    What are the top three items you would like to
    see on your vision board?

    _____

    _____

    _____

Thoughts Around Vision

Vision is a vivid picture of the future which creates passion in the present - a picture of your preferred future. - Steve Gutzler

Where there is no vision, the people perish. – Proverbs 29:18

Good business leaders create a vision, articulate the vision, and relentlessly drive it to completion. – Jack Welch

People buy into the leader before they buy into the vision. – John C. Maxwell

A dream is your creative vision for your life in the future. You must break out of your current comfort zone and become comfortable with the unfamiliar and the unknown. – Denis Waitley

You know you have a vision when you are willing to cry, fight, and claw for what you believe. – Steve Gutzler

Forget about trying to compete with someone else. Create your own pathway. Create your own new vision. – Herbie Hancock

Britain's goal is not to survive, but to prevail. – Sir Winston Churchill

It's never too late to be what you might have been. – George Eliot

Chapter 4: Courage

"It takes courage to realize your dreams and to give meaning to your values." - James M. Kouzes

Let's Soar!

"Dad, if we are going to do it, let's go to 1,600 feet!" - Jayce Gutzler

If you have been to the Caribbean or parts of Mexico, you are quite familiar with parasailing. From the beach it looks peaceful, with the colorful sail gliding through blue sky being pulled by one of those "Miami Vice" type speed boats. Awesome – let's do that!

In reality, it's nerve-racking. The water is choppy. The drivers of our boat seemed to be suspiciously sipping tequila. The cables looked shaky. The harness straps creep up into places they shouldn't creep. Sure, it looked peaceful from the beach but once you got out there, suddenly everything seemed so much more difficult and intimidating!

Once you arrive at the liftoff point, they ask, "How high do you want to go?"

The options are for 800 feet, 1,200 feet, or a terrifying 1,600 feet.

I was thinking that 800 sounded like a good option for me. I'm not really a big fan of heights or tight harnesses or choppy waters.

But before I could say anything, my son, Jayce, answered, "Dad, if we are going to do it, let's go for 1,600 feet!"

I was the last of my family to sail. I watched my three kids and my wife all take their turns flying above the water. I listened to their laughter, their screams, and the shouts of excitement. I watched their faces, their wide eyes, and their big smiles. All of this encouraged me to give it my best shot. I do have a serious fear of heights, so this was a huge deal for me!

When I got up there, it was brilliant. It was breathtaking. It was so amazing to finally SOAR!

What about you?

Is there a part of you that has settled comfortably on the beach of life? When was the last time you looked your fears in the eye and told them that they are not going to keep you down any longer? When was the last time you stretched yourself? When was the last time you looked yourself in the eyes and said, "If I'm going to do it, I'm going to go 1,600 feet"?

Discover your Brilliance

This is your chance to take what you have and find that extra degree of sparkle.

In my coaching and corporate speaking, I typically issue a leadership challenge to everyone I speak with:

First: Set targets in life and business that are high – 1,600-feet high! Get off the lounge chair and dream big, think big, and get crystal clear about defined goals and greatness. Set your targets to stretch you even higher than you can imagine!

Second: Start listening to your "Big Voice" that drives your subconscious and mind and, in turn, determines your conscious actions. Transform your thoughts through inspirational readings, books, and messages. Read to lead – personal development books, futuristic books, soul-based books, and spiritual books. Your mind and thoughts are key to igniting positive emotions. And remember, emotions drive our behaviors and performance!

Third: Move toward that which you fear. I used to be afraid of ultra-success. "Just give me a little," I would think. But I had to break that meager and small-minded thought. To do that, I set a big, stretch, fear-defying goal this year – double my business and double my influence in one year.

Sometimes you have to challenge yourself. You have to risk it, you have to write it, and you have to say it!

Now, if I get there I might go back to Mexico and celebrate. Maybe I'll even sail again!

The Determined Dreamer

Question: Where have you been tempted to give up?

Question: Have you thought about tossing your dream to the wind?

Question: Can you look at one man's life and be inspired to begin again?

If you can, take a look at some of this man's accomplishments:

- A man instrumental in bringing an end to slavery
- A man responsible for writing and delivering one of our nation's most famous speeches, The Gettysburg Address
- A man that guided a nation through its single greatest test – the Civil War
- A man for which history stands in awe

Look at the scoreboard of his life! He actually had a losing record in life:

1. He had a very difficult childhood and was raised in incredible poverty.

2. He had less than one year of formal schooling.

3. 1831: He entered his first business: It failed.

4. 1832: He ran for public office: He was defeated.

5. 1833: He started another business: It failed.

6. 1834: He ran for public office: He won!

7. 1835: The girl he was about to marry died suddenly.

8. 1838: He was defeated as Speaker.

9. 1840: He was defeated as Elector.

10. 1842: He was married to Mary Todd. They had four sons. Only one son lived past the age of 18 years old. The other boys died at ages 4, 11, and 18.

11. 1843: He again ran for Congress: He was defeated.

12. 1846: He was elected to Congress!

13. 1848: He was defeated for Congress.

14. 1855: He was defeated for Senate.

15. 1856: He was defeated for Vice President.

16. 1858: He was defeated for Senate again.

Let me ask you: If that were your scorecard, would you have run for president? Fortunately for our nation, Abraham Lincoln did.

Three lessons from Lincoln:

1. He was resilient and always pushed through quitting points. You can, too!

2. He was known for his ability to build bridges with people who earlier had opposed him.

3. He believed that failure is not an outcome but an attitude. Choose to have a successful attitude!

My Favorite Lincoln Quote:

"I do not like that man. I must get to know him better."

I encourage you this day to step back and rethink any setback or perceived failure you have had. It truly is preparing you for the magnificent purpose for which you were created.

Be determined in your dreams!

Just the First Step

It was my best shot. My mom had gone to Ernie's Grocery Store and I was home alone. My palms were sweaty, my throat was dry, and my fingers were shaking as I dialed our old manual telephone. My greatest fear was that Mr. Olsen would answer. My second greatest fear at the moment was that Nancy wouldn't remember who I was. After all, I went to Cedar Park Junior High and she attended Meadow Park Junior High.

I had met Nancy a few weeks earlier at a combined school dance. They called it a sock-hop. I didn't have the courage to ask her to dance then. But now, by golly, I was going to take the first step! The first step is always the hardest! I was calling her up! I'd never called a girl before. I had rehearsed it over and over in my mind. As I dialed it was both exciting and excruciating ... 664-2734 ... ring ... ring ... ring ...

The deepest, lowest voice I have ever heard answered, "Hello?" I was pretty sure that wasn't Nancy. I was pretty sure it was Mr. Olsen. My greatest fear realized!

I stammered out the words "... Hi Mr. Olsen. This is Steve Gutzer. Is Nancy there?" Then the deep voice again, "Yes!" A pause ... "Um, may I please speak with her?" My voice was not deep; instead, it was cracking, breaking,

imploding! Then he said in that deep voice ... "Sure, Steve."
Magical words! Just those two words rang like success!

When Nancy came to the phone, I felt emboldened and
empowered. We had the most amazing and thought-
provoking conversation. We talked about weird teachers,
funny friends, her new shoes, my old shoes and we
laughed!

As a 13-year-old kid, that was a breakthrough!

It was JUST THE FIRST STEP!

I know it is a childhood example, but it isn't childish! I
am around a lot of leaders, a lot of entrepreneurs, and a lot
of business types. Some of these people carry a bundle of
precious dreams around in their hearts, but that is just the
problem! The dreams are only carried around in their
hearts! They are afraid of taking that first step. They are
afraid of deep-voiced Mr. Olsen saying, "No, you cannot
talk to Nancy."

I heard Les Brown say recently, "Let me tell you a little
secret – you're not coming out alive in life! You will either
be in the grandstands or on the playing field. You might as
well get on the field and start playing!"

The Stuff that Dreams Are Made of:

1. <u>What are you waiting for?</u> Perfect conditions?
   Less stress? Slower pace? Freed up schedule?
   There is no such thing as perfect conditions and
   probably, things are not going to slow down
   much.
2. <u>What is holding you back?</u> Which fear? Is it the
   fear of failure? The fear of the unknown? As you
   move toward that which you fear, it will grow
   smaller, not larger! Your momentum and traction
   will gain speed and soon whatever fear has held
   you captive will be tamed by your activity, not
   your passivity.

3. <u>How do you get started?</u> In your overworked and imperfect state, you start with just the first step. Your first step may be small at first, but it will be impactful in the long run.

"That is one small step for man, one giant leap for mankind." – Neil Armstrong

"All our dreams can come true if we have the courage to pursue them."

– Steve Gutzler

Questions to Build Momentum in: Courage

1.   Can you courageously identify two to three areas where you have comfortably settled on the "beach" of life?

_____

_____

_____

_____

2. Where do you need to stretch in your personal leadership?

_____

_____

_____

_____

3. Where in life have you always wanted to soar – financially, relationally, spiritually, recreationally?

_____

_____

_____

_____

4.   What lesson can you learn from Lincoln in regard to courage and determination?

_____

_____

_____

_____

5.   What is one step you can take today to push a dream forward?

_____

_____

_____

_____

Thoughts Around Courage

Success is not final, failure is not fatal: It is the courage to continue that counts. – Winston Churchill

Your time is limited, so don't waste it living someone else's life. Have the courage to follow your heart and intuition. – Steve Jobs

All our dreams can come true if we have the courage to pursue them. – Walt Disney

Take chances, make mistakes. That's how you grow. Pain nourishes your courage. You have to fail in order to practice being brave. – Mary Tyler Moore

Courage, guts, sacrifice, determination, faith, commitment, toughness, grit, heart, soul, and talent. That's what leaders are made of. – Steve Gutzler

He who is not courageous enough to take risks will accomplish nothing in life. – Mohammad Ali

America was not built on fear. America was built on courage, on imagination and an unbeatable determination to do the job at hand. – Harry S. Truman

Courage is resistance to fear, mastery of fear, not absence of fear. – Mark Twain

Chapter 5: Determination

"Don't compare yourself – strive to complete yourself. We are all on a journey." – Steve Gutzler

Determined Visualization

"It was not the fatigue or even the cold water that defeated me." – Florence Chadwick

When she looked ahead, Florence Chadwick saw nothing but a solid wall of fog. Her body was numb. She had been swimming for more than 16 hours.

At 34, she wanted to be the first woman to swim from Catalina Island to the California coast. It was 1952 and millions watched Florence on national television as she struggled in the frigid cold waters and dense fog. Her support boats with her trainer and mother encouraged her to continue on. Sharks cruised toward her body, only to be driven away by rifle shots.

They told her it wasn't much farther; they urged her not to give up. But all she could see was fog. With less than half a mile to shore, she quit.

Several hours later in front of a cluster of reporters, she said: "It was not the fatigue or even the cold water that defeated me. It was the fog. I was unable to see my goal."

Two months later, she tried again. This time, despite the same dense fog, she swam with her faith intact and her dream clearly pictured in her mind.

She knew that somewhere beyond the fog was land. And this time she made it! She became the first woman to swim the Catalina Channel, and she even eclipsed the previous men's time by two hours!

What is your dream?

1. **You may know it in your heart and mind ...**
   ... but you must visualize it clearly, for the fog and the frigid waters of resistance are coming your way. Picture completion. Picture the finish line. It may be a big project like a new business opportunity, a meaningful relationship, or a healthy body. Get your vision in crystal-clear living color. Lock it in!

2. **Just know everyone, everywhere, experiences the fog.**
   There is one thing more powerful than the dense fog – a determined dreamer. You might be in a foggy funk right now, but do not worry. You are not alone. Each of us hits a wall sometimes, but stay encouraged and ...

3. **Try again!**
   I love the fact that Florence climbed back into those waters just two months later. You, too, can start again if you are stopped the first time.

You can begin again!

Your dream is not too big for you!

Sometimes when we push through the quitting points, the fog will lift and we will see land. No matter where you find yourself, TRY AGAIN! All people have experienced failure, but only great people will get up and try again despite their failures.

Come on – keep swimming!

Choosing to Prevail

As a little boy, he would often cry himself to sleep at night. In the sixth grade at a boarding school in England, he struggled painfully with his studies and was hopelessly failing. During recess, he would run into the woods and hide because the other boys would relentlessly tease him. They said he had a head that was too big!

Finally, one day the school master sent a note home to his mother. It simply read, **"Your boy shows a conspicuous lack of success."** His mother used it as a tool for motivation instead of humiliation.

Years later, this little boy had grown into Sir Winston Churchill. He waved that very same note as he was sworn in as Prime Minister of the British people twice (1940-1945 and 1951-1955).

He became the "Voice of Hope" to the British people in World War II and a great world leader who took on Hitler and the evils of Nazi Germany. In one of his great speeches he said, "Everyone is asking on the streets, 'How will the British people survive?' We are asking the wrong question. It's not how will we survive, but how will we prevail?"

He taught the British people to have a prevailing spirit!

What about your personal leadership?

• Has someone tried to pin a note on you saying something like, "... a conspicuous lack of success?"

• Has a so-called failure or setback in your business or relationship convinced you to devalue your personal worth?

I HOPE NOT!

It is time to shift!

Simply put, let those "small voices" fire you up. Shift from surviving to prevailing! Churchill hit the pinnacle of leadership in his 60s and 70s. It is not too late for you or me!

I remember how more than 25 years ago, I was about to move my little family to Seattle to start my life over. I had a leader I respected deeply tell me, "Steve, you are making a big mistake. It is too risky. Don't do it." He chuckled as he told me I would be a "casualty."

It was exactly what I needed to hear because it fired me up! There were some tough and turbulent times. We didn't know a soul and we were lonely. But years later, Seattle is home and we love it. I am grateful to have established a prevailing leadership company teaching other organizations to prevail! I have new lifelong friends and scores of great memories, with plenty more to be made. The leader who gave me the negative advice has since passed away. But I still owe him a lot. That was my Churchill moment – and you can have one too.

"I have nothing to offer but blood, toil, tears, and sweat." - Winston Churchill

"Success is not final; failure is not fatal. It is courage to continue that counts." - Winston Churchill

If I Get to Five

Naomi was only four when she arrived at Beth Israel Hospital in New York City. She had a complicated brain tumor that was wrapped around two arteries. This was more than 25 years ago and pediatric neurosurgery was still in its infancy.

Dr. Fred Epstein, the founding director of the Institute for Neurology and Neurosurgery (INN) at Beth Israel Hospital in New York City, was commissioned to remove Naomi's tumor over the course of two delicate surgeries that were both deemed "a long shot."

After Naomi survived the first surgery, this feisty girl with dancing eyes and a bandaged head pronounced:

"If I get to five, I'm going to learn how to ride a two-wheeler!"

Then each day leading up to the next surgery, as Dr. Epstein made his rounds, there was Naomi making her bold statements:

Monday: If I get to five, I'm going to beat my older brother at tic-tac-toe!

Tuesday: If I get to five, I'm going learn to tie my shoes in double knots!

Wednesday: If I get to five, I'm going to learn to jump rope backwards!

What Dr. Epstein was learning from this courageous little 4-year old girl was:

1. You can draw courage from a 4-year-old.
2. Courage is greater than fear.
3. She knew that getting to five was an "if" and not a "when" proposition.

Naomi understood that in order to get to five years old, she needed to look forward to the next level of mastery, like learning to tie her shoes in double knots or learning to jump rope backwards.

Naomi survived both surgeries and although there was some brain damage, her courage has sustained her. She has since stayed very close to Dr. Epstein, and Dr. Epstein told her story (and many others) in his book *If I Get to Five: What Children Can Teach Us About Courage and Character*.

Exceptional You 2.0 Question

How are you doing with determination to embrace the next stages of your life?

To get to that next level and next stage in business and leadership, it will require the pursuit and mastery of new skills.

Naomi reminds us that even when "inoperable" is stamped across our lives, we need to strengthen our resolve to never give up. She was determined to make it to five so that she could learn new skills. We must strengthen our resolve to never give up in dire situations – not on a child, not on a relationship, not on our business, and especially not on our dreams, no matter how daunting the next challenge is. Just go for it!

I am sure if you are like me, life can get pretty messy and mundane at times. At other times, it can become overwhelming and burdensome.

But children, like the elderly, can teach us about courage and character. For one thing, children live life in the moment. They usually take on just today. Remember, today matters! And the elderly don't have the strength to live much more beyond today. Like my Grandma Gutzler used to tell me, "I am just happy to be alive today."

Six Take-Away Truths from Naomi and Dr. Epstein:

1. Hold someone's hand.
   "We can do no great things. Only small things with great love." – Mother Teresa
2. Live in the moment.
   "The best thing about the future is that it comes one day at a time." – Abraham Lincoln
3. Face your fears.
   "Courage is not the absence of fear, but rather the judgment that something else is more important than fear." – Ambrose Redmoon
4. Believe in miracles.
   "Sometimes, children teach us character, other times they teach us childlike truth which leads to miracles." – Steve Gutzler (hey, I know him!)
5. Play your strengths.

"I don't think I shall easily bow down before the blows that inevitably come to everyone." – Anne Frank

6. Love without boundaries.

   "Now I know I've got a heart because it is breaking." – Tin Woodman from *The Wizard of Oz*

Today matters. Live it with fresh courage, faith, and childlike determination.

Questions to Build Momentum in: Determination

1. Florence Chadwick tried to achieve her goal after her first attempt failed. Where can you attempt again, turning failure into a friend on your journey to success?

_____

_____

_____

2. Winston Churchill used a difficult childhood experience to fuel his motivation. What one setback can you use to motivate you?

_____

_____

_____

3. Winston Churchill reached the pinnacle of his career in his 60s and 70s. What lesson can you draw from him in bringing patience to your determination?

_____

_____

_____

4. What does Naomi's "If I get to five" mantra teach us about overcoming great odds?

_____

_____

_____

Thoughts Around Determination

A dream doesn't become a reality through magic; it takes sweat, determination, and hard work. – Colin Powell

Failure will never overtake me if my determination to succeed is strong enough. – Og Mandino

Desire is the key to motivation, but it's determination and commitment to an unrelenting pursuit of your goal – a commitment to excellence – that will enable you to attain the success you seek. – Mario Andretti

The difference between the impossible and the possible lies in a man's determination. – Tommy Lasorda

Never underestimate a man or woman who has a fire in their soul to succeed. A determination to push through quitting points. – Steve Gutzler

The truest wisdom is a resolute determination. – Napoleon Bonaparte

Success means having the courage, the determination, and the will to become the person you believe you were meant to be. – George A. Sheehan

If you set goals and go after them with all the determination you can muster, your gifts will take you places that will amaze you. – Les Brown

Chapter 6: Resiliency

"Everyone has hurt and pain from their past; the key is to learn and grow forward!" – Steve Gutzler

The Stuff that Dreams Are Made Of

Remember the lyrics from that Carly Simon song, "The Stuff that Dreams Are Made Of"? Personally, my dream started in brokenness. Things had been progressing pretty well. I had a wonderful wife, a nice house, and three kids that brought me joy and abundance. But then suddenly, I was out of work. It only ended up lasting a few months but I had found so much self-identity, self-esteem, and self-concept in my work that it quickly brought me to ground zero.

The low point was looking through the Seattle Times Classifieds and interviewing over the phone for a sales position. I was being interviewed by the sales director who was probably a few years my junior, had low emotional intelligence, and had poor interviewing skills for a position that was definitely below my pay grade.

This is the part of the story of which I am not proud. I hung up on him mid-sentence. I felt degraded, devalued, and humiliated. It wasn't his fault, but my own. I was in a freefall of identity and purpose. Just hours prior to the interview, I had parked my car in an empty parking lot to despair and to weep for a couple hours. Looking back, I don't know if I was clinically depressed, but it felt that way. I would try desperately to pull to the surface only to slide back down.

Fast forward a few months.

On a walk with my new golden retriever puppy, Rosie, I heard the whisper. The Creator Himself said to me, "Your life is not over. We are just getting started!" I referenced this earlier, but I still get chills when I think about it. I am so grateful for that voice and for that nudge when God reminded me that my job did not determine who I am, and reminded me that I am not a failure, and that I am not a "no count."

It was there in the back trails of our neighborhood that I birthed the dream for Leadership Quest.

The growth chart of my company has not been strictly up and to the right. Instead, it has been ebb and flow. But I now walk with confidence and smile. I so desperately want people to feel the possibility of purpose, to feel the exhilaration of the pursuit of that one big thing.

I would like to offer three points from Carly Simon's lyrics for you to really ponder:

1. **It is your heart and soul's desire:** Can you slow enough to listen to your heart beat? To listen to your soul's desire? To your dream?

2. **Don't look at yourself in the same old way. Take a new picture:** Oh, if I could help you take a new picture of yourself and your dream! I want to help you discover a fresh perspective.

3. **It is the reason we are alive!** It is not hard for me to say I wept in my car for over two hours because I thought my best days were over. But I made a comeback. And it didn't consume me. Instead, it recast me into the man – with an extraordinary dream – I am today.

When Good Things Go Bad

Surprise – I'm a channel surfer. As in, give me the remote and let's see what is on every one of the 500 channels I have on my TV. And let's do it as fast as we can. Jewelry ad, sports, news, news, news, Sesame Street, news, sports, sports, sports, reality TV, soap, soap, Hispanic, cartoon, cartoon, cartoon, Judge Judy, cartoon, reality, reality, National Geographic, sports, sports, history, Sci-Fi, Sports, reality, reality ... wow!

In the rare moments that I get to sit down and turn on the ol' tube, I surf. Knowing I only have a few minutes, I never commit to a long story. I like it best when I come across those reality shows like "When Good Things Go Bad." I love those quick episodes of people running with the bulls in Spain when suddenly one guy is trapped and the bulls have him cornered. Once, I saw a couple at a wedding walking down the aisle when they tripped and fell backwards into a fountain! All right! There is some quality TV! That is worth my time! If I am committing to 15 minutes, I want a crash scene, a fight scene, a funny scene or a love scene – maybe all at once.

But life isn't channel surfing.

(Or maybe it is ... Twitter, Facebook ...)

But in real life, sometimes good things really do go bad.

I'm not a prophet of doom. I am positive and have learned the power of optimism. But from time to time, good things in relationships and business go bad.

Here is a quick reminder if you are facing a bad time: It could turn into a good time!

Practice Framing

Whether in a personal or business challenge, it is your responsibility as a leader to "frame" a mental picture of the situation here and now. Use pictures and symbols to define reality. You can frame the situation or others will. You can let it slide and it will go from bad to worse!

Steps for Framing

1. Control the Context: You can't always control events, but get out in front and control the way they are understood by others. This is very important if you lead an organization.

2. Define the Situation: Give a mental model to others where you connect them in a meaningful way. Create a culture of "sense-making" where people are motivated to choose a right path, not a destructive one.

3. Be Courageous: Communicate clearly and honestly. Do not be afraid of personal or team "open-audit times." The revealing of feelings can be the beginning of healing and restoration of a bad time or challenging setback. Be courageous and start right away!

4. Interpret Uncertainty: To reduce uncertainty, choose a leadership moment. Remember Giuliani taking charge in New York City after September 11. There was a lot of turbulence and uncertainty, but it felt reassuring when he took charge with honest clarity to interpret our uncertainty.

5. Design the Response: The toughest time to lead yourself and others is during deep challenge. You may not know all of the winds and the waves coming at you, but you can set a course. The moment you choose to get engaged and tackle your problem, you will feel empowered. The victim mentality will be powerfully replaced by the victor's mindset. Start designing your "First Seven Days Response."

6. Manage Your Emotions: Emotions drive behaviors. Good leaders learn to self-manage their emotions. Just last week, I had a courageous conversation. It was a conference call that I knew was going to be challenging and had a high potential to emotionally hijack me! I wrote four big letters on a sheet in front of me: "CALM." I knew a lot was at stake and staying calm was my most significant leadership assignment. I needed a win/win outcome, not an "I Win, You Lose" outcome.

When good things go bad, try the powerful steps of "Framing."

Undaunted Courage

"Hang on a minute, guys. Don't come up yet. I have a little surprise for you." - John Ortberg

Undaunted Courage is Stephen Ambrose's best-selling account of the Lewis and Clark expedition. Our family has a little beach cabin in Seaside, Oregon, where the expedition concluded. They have one of those really cool statues commemorating the expedition at a turnaround point that looks out on the Pacific Ocean.

Throughout the expedition, they battled nearly insurmountable challenges, including hunger, severe illness, fatigue, desertion, hostile enemies, and death (not your average road trip across the country). Then, the team finally reached the headwaters of the Missouri River. All advance information had led them to believe that this meant they were also close to the Columbia River which would be a gentle float safely westward to the Pacific Ocean. They would be heroes at last!

Meriwether Lewis went ahead to climb a bluff to view the picturesque waters. Imagine what he felt when rather than seeing a gentle sloping valley, he saw the majestic and intimidating Rocky Mountains.

Question To Leaders:

• What do you do when you think your biggest challenges are behind you – only to find out you were just warming up?

• How do you rally yourself?

• How do you rally your troops?

I picture Lewis motioning the rest of the party to stay behind while he figured out how he was going to break the news about the trek up the mountains.

Maybe he said something like, "Hang on a minute, guys. Don't come up yet. I have a little surprise for you."

Eventually, crossing the Rocky Mountains would be the supreme challenge and supreme achievement. It called forth enormous creativity, innovation, and perseverance. It led them to spectacular sights and unforgettable memories. It built an inner confidence because when you know you can tackle the Rocky Mountains, you know you can tackle anything!

What Is Your Rocky Mountain Challenge?

- Finding new customers or business clients?
- New upgrades to brand and marketing?
- New innovations or new service offerings?
- New projects with fast-approaching deadlines?
- New personal confidence to tackle your work?
- New strength to continue upward?

When you start climbing and stretching and sweating, you will find the way to climb, new ideas, and breakthrough innovation in your work. You will find the stamina you need to go higher. You will meet new people and discover new clients. You will discover your inner strength and awaken your Undaunted Courage.

Come on – let's climb together! You and me! Let's make it to the Pacific Ocean!

"Remember it's the finish, not the start, which counts the most in life."

— John C. Maxwell

Questions to Build Momentum in: Resiliency

1. Where in your life can look back and be grateful you didn't quit?

_____

_____

_____

2. What did you learn from that experience? How can that serve you in building momentum?

_____

_____

_____

_____

3. What is one "Rocky Mountain" challenge you will face in the next 12 months?

_____

_____

_____

4. How will you reframe it as an opportunity to gain new energy?

_____

_____

_____

Thoughts Around Resiliency

Be faithful in small things because it is in them that your strength lies. – Mother Teresa

Never lose faith in the end of your story. – Steve Gutzler

Man never made any material as resilient as the human spirit. – Bernard Williams

Women are tough, women are resilient, and have an underlying hope. – Katherine McNamara

One thing about championship teams is that they're resilient. No matter what is thrown at them, no matter how deep the hole, they find a way to bounce back and overcome adversity. – Nick Saban

People make mistakes all the time. We learn and grow. If there's patience and love, and you care for people, you can work them through it, and they can find their greatest heights. – Pete Carroll

Grit is that 'extra something' that separates the most successful people from the rest. It's the passion, perseverance, and stamina that we must channel in order to stick with our dreams until they become a reality. – Travis Bradberry

Chapter 7: Rejuvenation

"Let's not take ourselves too seriously. Let's enjoy the ride!" – Robin Sharma

I Dropped the Wedding Cake

"Steve, do us a big favor. We need you to run to the bakery and pick up the wedding cake. Be back in 30 minutes!"

I love challenging assignments. And I've always been a team player. This wedding was definitely a team effort. The couple being wed were my dear friends and I was commissioned to go to the local bakery and pick up the cake. I needed to be back ASAP. I drove off humming, "Going to the chapel and they're going to get married ... " I was in a great mood and excited to see these two people begin their lives together.

Then, upon receiving the cake, I headed back to my car. The weirdest thing happened ... I tripped. I didn't stumble; I full-out tripped on the curb. It felt like a slow motion belly flop into the road, and the big box holding the cake flew out of my hands into the air ... it turned one-and-a-half giant turns and landed. Up. Side. Down.

My mind started racing. It was one of those moments where you wonder if what is happening is actually happening, and pray that it isn't. I peeled back the lid of the box ... all the icing was stuck to the top. The two wedding bells looked up at me like demonic faces. I was dazed. I was confused. Now what? I was in one big wedding cake mess!

As I sheepishly carried the mushed box into the reception area preparing my last remarks, a woman greeted me saying, "Wonderful – the cake! I bet it's lovely!"

I looked down at the box, down at my feet, up at the ceiling, then at her, "Actually, I dropped the sucker."

You won't believe what happened next. This may be even more amazing than the slow motion cake-kerplop. The woman at the reception was a premiere cake designer, a frosting expert, a cake CPR genius extraordinaire. She said, "How about we give this a little make over?" I nodded, thinking it was probably going to be more like a reconstruction. Within minutes she began to recreate, redecorate, and restore the cake's beauty. Lo and behold – it looked good as new! Better than new! An amazing new beginning! The cake got a fresh start!

What does a Fresh Start look like for you?

So many of my clients and friends need a fresh start. It is like they have taken a tumble and don't know how to start getting up.

I would like to offer seven things you can do today to imagine your fresh start:

1. Come up with a "one-day plan."

When I get stuck, overwhelmed, stressed or broken, I go back to the basics and live one day at a time. Just map out today. Don't bite off too much.

2. Get physical.

The stress hormone cortisol can create havoc in your mind and emotions and narrow your perspective really quickly. Even if you can't get to the gym, create your own 30-minute home workout. Put on some rocking music and get physical! It will generate positive hormones, natural highs, and boost your self-concept.

3. Focus on accomplishments.

Activities are flooding most people's busy days. To create a higher impact fresh start, focus on the 20 percent of your activities that give you 80 percent of your return in your work/life balance.

4. Don't isolate. Initiate!

Isolation is suffocating people. This world can become small and lonely. Get out there! Meet with that trusted friend or associate that brings you goodness, ideas, and health. Cultivate a rhythm of meeting with the best and the bright. You become who you associate with. Associate with winners!

5. Eat to win.

You don't have to be a health nut but pick good food choices that fuel your days. Try things like cut veggies, raw almonds, cranberries, or whole wheat crackers. Double your water intake. And try some new natural supplements. Build your immune system daily and your moods will level out as well. And you will rarely be sick!

6. Unplug one day a week.

Sounds impossible, right? Wrong. The primary downfall I see with technology and social media is people have no start and no ending. No healthy breaks. Give your mind, your soul, and your spirit a break. Your family will like you a whole lot more, too! I unplug every Sunday and I love it!

7. Practice guilt-free rest.

When your body and mind say, "I need a break," don't push through every time. Treat your body like a temple, like the precious gift it is. Allow for your human limitations. Allow yourself to let go and relax and recover. Grant yourself permission for a fresh start!

Let Go of the Purse!

I'm not a big outdoors guy. Don't get me wrong – I live in the Pacific Northwest and love the Puget Sound waters, the

Cascade Mountains, and Mt. Rainier. But I don't much care to camp, hunt or fish. Part of my issue is just that I was never brought up doing those things. So the few times that I have ventured out, I am like Billy Crystal in *City Slickers*.

Now, my late father-in-law Chuck was an all-American outdoorsman. He looked like John Wayne and Clint Eastwood rolled into one manly man. He didn't talk much and he loved to hunt and fish.

So one day several years ago, we found ourselves in a fishing boat – just the two of us in this little boat. Did I mention that he didn't talk much? An older couple anchored nearby in their little aluminum boat. From where we were anchored, I could see all the equipment they had in that little boat, and remember thinking, "That is another reason that I don't like fishing! All that gear!"

And then it happened. The older gentleman stood up in the boat to rearrange something and in an instant, the boat had flipped over and was on top of the couple who were now in the water. You could hear them pounding beneath the boat. Chuck and I quickly pulled up our anchor and started racing over to help.

By the time we arrived, the man was holding onto the side of the boat. But we could see the woman through the clear water sinking towards the bottom. It was a slow-motion scene, like an eerie horror film.

Inspired by episodes of *Baywatch* I'd seen, I dove into the water to rescue this old woman who was about 10 feet under by this time. I grabbed her by the shirt and started pulling her to the surface – except it felt like she weighed a thousand pounds! I thought water was supposed to make you feel lighter! It was a major struggle for me to get her to the surface. When I finally did, I realized why it had felt like I was trying to surface a whale: SHE HAD BEEN HOLDING ONTO HER PURSE.

I kid you not. And this was no small clutch. This was more like a parachute purse. And it acted just like a parachute, filling with water instead of air.

Now, I know that women have a personal attachment to their purses ... but come on! Let it go!

It's a silly-but-true story. Honestly, I have been thinking about what I need to let go of these days. I cling to so many things in my life and leadership business that I think are so important but in reality, they may be taking me down or holding me back from true greatness!

Here are my "Let Go" and "Hold On" Lists for these days:

"Let Go" of ...

1. Feeling that I need to "control" other people
2. Any destructive habit holding me down from reaching the surface of my dreams
3. Dishonest corners of my soul
4. Being wired to technology to the point where I ignore daily soul nourishment
5. Any platform of self-promotion to boost ego
6. Any "purse" filled with tons of activities not aligned with my greater purpose
7. Any habit that is not uplifting or healthy
8. Feelings of guilt when I rest and recover
9. Isolation from my leadership community
10. Judgment of others and playing small
11.

"Hold On" to ...

1. Times of solitude, reading and reflection
2. Leaders who lift me by meeting one at a time

3. Relationships that matter with family and trusted friends
4. Giving freely with no expectation of return
5. Balanced diet and exercise even when no one is looking
6. God
7. My purpose and calling that is uniquely me
8. Being a leader to my family and modeling consistently to those I am privileged to lead
9. Blueprinting my week around accomplishments, not activities
10. Wisdom and work that nourish life in others

Exceptional You 2.0

Can you push away from the sounds and noise? Can you, for a few moments, disconnect and take time to make your authentic list of what to "LET GO" of and what to "HOLD ON" to?

Leaders are honest, but they are also human. Sometimes, we need time to recalibrate our lives around what matters most!

"Fear nothing except to waste precious moments. Look to every day as a new day and make each day better than the last." - Steve Gutzler

Questions to Build Momentum in: Rejuvenation

1. Where can you allow yourself a fresh start? Physically, emotionally, mentally?

_____

_____

_____

_____

2. What 20 percent of your work provides 80 percent of the return? How can you rejuvenate that 20 percent?

_____

_____

_____

_____

3. Where have you been tempted to isolate? Can you initiate some new relationships or network possibilities?

_____

_____

_____

_____

4. Can you take time to generate your own "let go" and "hang on" list?

_____

_____

_____

_____

Thoughts Around Rejuvenation

My purpose is to inspire greatness in others – to refuel, refresh, restore, and rejuvenate leaders. – Steve Gutzler

I take conscious breaks for myself 'cause I like to rejuvenate and get my creative juices flowing. I also like to take my time with my creativity; I think it's important. – Brandy Norwood

It's important to just kind of get away from your sport until you miss it. It's about taking time to enjoy other aspects of life or learn new things. It helps me rejuvenate. – Misty May-Treanor

Becoming a grandmother brought me back to things I forgot to love. Nature. Playing, seeing animals. A new way of looking. A rejuvenation. A cycle of life – things come back to you. The details. – Carine Roitfield

I restore myself when I'm alone. – Marilyn Monroe

What rejuvenates me? Humor, humility, excitement, creativity, fulfillment, honesty, passion, hard work, rest, and love! – Steve Gutzler

How do you spell rejuvenation? Rec-re-a-tion-al activites. – Unknown

Chapter 8: Brevity

"Deep in our soul, each of us knows there will never be a better time to live our biggest life." - Steve Gutzler

Promises

"I told the other kids not to worry. I told them that if you were alive, you'd save me ..." - Jim Burns

The 1989 Armenian earthquake needed only four minutes to flatten a nation and kill more than 30,000 people. Moments after the deadly tremor was over, a father raced to the nearby elementary school to save his son. Looking at the masses of rubble and stone, he remembered a promise he had made to his child, "No matter what happens, I will always be there for you."

Standing and sobbing with the other parents, he decided to start digging. He began to remove one giant stone at a time. The authorities urged him to stop. They said, "It is too late. They are all gone."

But the man refused to stop. For eight hours, then 16, then 36 hours, he dug. His hands were raw and his energy drained. But he refused to quit.

Finally, after 38 exhausting hours of blood, sweat and tears, he heard a faint voice ... "Arman, Arman! Daddy! It's me!" Then the boy uttered the words that should give each leader pause:

"I told the other kids not to worry. I told them that if you were alive, you'd save me. And when you saved me, they would be saved, too. Because you promised, 'No matter what happens, I will always be there for you.'"*

*(Story excerpted from *Uncommon Stories and Illustrations* by Jim Burns)

Promises Made, Promises Kept

It begins with soulful honesty.

• Remember your promises as a leader, big and small.
• Remember to trust in the foundation of leadership and personal influence.
• Ask yourself: Is there any rubble that you need to remove?
• Ask yourself: Where do you need to keep your word?
• What are the promises you have made to yourself you need to keep?

Leadership is being a man or woman of your word. It's fighting for others that we love. It's doing the work that others say cannot be done.

"Leadership is an affair of the heart because we love those we lead." - Steve Gutzler

"Sometimes you have to push through quitting points to save others." - Steve Gutzler

What Matters Most

"Someone altered the script. My lines have changed. I thought I was writing the play." - Madeleine L'Engle

Have you ever had a day where things click? I honestly couldn't recall a more productive day. I woke with energy, blueprinted my day, cleaned my office, found 20 bucks (yahoo!), and I had provided coaching for outstanding clients around leadership attributes of world-class leaders. I was clicking!

And then at exactly 6:45 p.m. on Highway 405 while I was driving home from Seattle, I received the call.

"Steve, this is Cynthia. Lee has had a stroke."

My mind was swirling. How could this be? Lee is my trainer and good friend. I just recently saw him as he was putting the finishing touches on competing in the Emerald Cup bodybuilding competition. Lee is a model of health. When you spend time with your trainer each week, you become close. Lee and I are close. Often, we find ourselves on a Saturday afternoon watching football. He only allows me to "eat clean," a phrase that I have adopted into my daily life. He reminds me to be a corporate athlete.

Lee had recently experienced the pain of having a son pass away. We had sat together in silence and wept. Friendship is forged strongest in pain and loss and trial.

Once again, my well-orchestrated life had slowed and fallen off beat. It crawled to a stop. I visited him in the hospital and have been walking with him through his journey the best I can. (He's now doing well. It appears he will recover with good care and rehab, for which we thank God!)

My Leadership Audit:

Lee is teaching me what matters most. Some lessons are harder to learn than others.

Questions I am thinking about in reflection to Lee's eye-opener:

1. How do I choose to invest my life? And with whom?

2. Am I really in control or do I need to take a step back and loosen my grip?

3. Can I slow down enough to follow simple promptings that matter? Relationships matter!

Note: I had thought of inviting Lee over for Easter brunch. I knew that he would have appreciated the invite, but I never got around to asking him. I have learned to prioritize the relationships in my life.

4. Can I still continue to build a calling of excellence all while keeping people in central view?

5. Can I restart my mission of "Inspiring Greatness in Others" with a new sense of urgency and passion?

6. Can I treat my one and only life as a gift and treat others with exemplary respect and love?

"Gratitude is the ability to experience life as a lovely gift. It liberates us from the prison of self-preoccupation." - John Ortberg

"I become smart when I get crystal clear on what lasts and what doesn't." - Steve Gutzler

Stop, Look, Listen

"I just almost got hit by a double-decker bus!"

I am a good leader, but I am not good when it comes to maps and locations. So it made perfect sense that my wife, Julie, took charge of mapping our three-day tourist trip to London.

Having just completed an extensive two-day leadership training to an extraordinary group of European Microsoft leaders, we were ready to hit the town.

We were armed with maps and hot coffees as we headed to the streets to catch the underground trains to our first attraction. Remember, I am a leader by nature so it was normal for me to stride out ahead. As we came to the first busy intersection, I looked left and saw that there were no cars coming. So I took a big step out to cross the street ...

One problem ...

Actually, a big problem ...

Vehicles don't approach from the left in London. They come from the right.

As you can imagine, I am not exaggerating when I tell you that as I took that step, I heard two very loud noises. One was a woman screaming (not my wife). The other was a blaring horn ... a blast from a red double-decker London bus.

I should be dead.

Flattened.

Pancaked.

Sitting on a cloud in a diaper playing a harp.

But, for whatever reason, I lunged backwards and the bus barely missed me. I could feel the wind and force of the bus next to my face. It was way too close for comfort. It was a near-death experience!

Thank God for that scream, the horn and the instinct to jump back. Otherwise, I would be nothing more than an American hood ornament.

The near death experience shook me. I tried to gather myself and play it cool, to shake it off. But the remainder of the day, I kept muttering, "I almost died ... I almost died ... I almost died ..."

It seemed like the rest of our trip I was in a perpetual state of reflection and was extra-tender about the gravity of life. It was the first time in a long time that I realized and really understood that someday I would die. Game over. I know it seems a bit heavy but honestly, I needed a wake-up call. I wasn't being cocky but I had forgotten how delicate, fragile, and finite life is. I had forgotten how life is a gift to us all.

My mentor, who I loved as much as you can love someone, died of leukemia. He told me once, "Steve, the difference between you and me is that you know you will die someday. I feel I am dying every day, so it is so real to me."

What can you learn from my near-miss?

1. **STOP:**
   We all need to stop and examine our lives, our purpose, our use of our one-and-only life. Ask yourself: *What is my ultimate goal and purpose?*
   I've concluded that a life well lived is one that is lived for others. I have a wife, three kids, six grandbabies, business associates, coaching clients and friends. Lord knows they need encouragement and inspiration. If I can play a role, even a little one, I am thrilled. I need a purpose-driven life!

2. **LOOK:**
   How much of your time is given to trivial pursuits? We need to look to leverage high-value accomplishments. Strive for greatness and extraordinary achievements. Do not settle for small stuff. Strike out toward the great things. Dreams we can and will reach with hard work and stunning faith! Look and adjust.

3. **LISTEN:**
   Listen to advice. Listen to those who have succeeded. Learn to lower the volume of small voices who emphasize weaknesses. Listen instead

to those voices that have put skin on their dreams and defied the naysayers. Listen to those who believe it is possible!

Honest and True Confession:

On the night we returned to the hotel, the night of my near death experience, I knelt by my bed like a child and thanked God that I didn't die. That Julie didn't have to feel that sadness or deal with details like how to get my body back to America. That God still felt fit to use me in this world. I promised God that I would follow His direction and allow Him to use me in whatever way He felt was best.

Remember – look both ways! You matter to me! Stop for a few moments to discover your purpose. Look at what matters most and adjust. Listen to that big voice preaching your accomplishments.

"Change in life starts when you see the next step and boldly take it."

– Steve Gutzler

Questions to Build Momentum in: Brevity

1. What are the promises you have made to yourself that you need to keep?

_____

_____

_____

_____

2. Can you build a calling of excellence while keeping people in central view?

_____

_____

_____

_____

3. How do you choose to invest your life? And with whom?

_____

_____

_____

_____

4. What are your top three priorities that you want to devote more time to?

_____

_____

_____

_____

Thoughts Around Brevity

Life really is a vapor. But if you live that vapor to the fullest, it becomes a splash! – Steve Gutzler

Life is worthwhile if you TRY. Try something to see if you can do it. Try something to make a difference. Try to make some progress. Try to learn a new skill. Try your best. Give it every effort. Life is worthwhile if you GIVE. Giving is better than receiving because giving starts the receiving process. Life is worthwhile if you BE. Wherever you are, be there. Develop a unique focus on the current moment. Let others lead small lives, but not you. Let other argue over small things, but not you. Let others cry over small hurts, but not you. Let others leave their futures in someone else's hands, but not you. – Jim Rohn

Chapter 9: Appreciation

"As you seek out the good in people, not only will they show up more fully for you but you will see more good in them." - Steve Gutzler

Others

"Mister, can I ask you a question? Are you an angel?"

When I boarded my flight to the Philippines several years ago, I wasn't in my "A+" attitude. Truth be told, I was in a bit of a cloudy funk. Nursing a ruptured disc in my lower back, I literally couldn't stand up for more than three minutes without feeling extreme pain. The thought of sitting on a plane for 20 hours ranked right up there with anticipating root canal surgery.

But I am a good soldier. As part of a team who had volunteered to help victims of sex trafficking, it was an essential trip to which I had made a commitment. So I was committed. Did I mention that it was August and 95 degrees with insane humidity? It felt like there were zillions of people everywhere in the smog. I stopped for a moment and focused myself on the goal. I sat there and reminded myself who I was and what I was doing.

The Night that Changed My World

On our fifth night of our trip, we had arranged to go directly into the "red-light district" to feed local prostitutes and provide hygiene packs. The proper arrangements were made and my local volunteers were also coming to help.

As we arrived in our little cabs, there they were. There were more than 150 moms, babies, and children lined up on the sidewalk. We served rice cups and passed out the hygiene packs. They were a group of truly grateful hearts and open souls.

One thin woman with a baby on her hip kept following me, brushing against me and looking into my eyes. I would smile and ask if she had everything she needed. I felt it was more of a sense of security she was searching for. She would look at me as a teenager would look to a father figure. After all, she was a teen mom and looked like she could have been my daughter.

Finally, having done all we could for the night, we headed back to the cabs, yet the young woman followed me. As I climbed in the car, she bent down and said the words that are forever burned in my soul:

"Mister, can I ask you a question? Are you an angel?"

I was speechless. I stammered out something along the lines of, "No honey, I am just a guy from Seattle here to let you know you are loved and that you matter to me." Simple words, but such inadequate words! As we drove back to our hotel, I put my head back against the seat. I asked God to forgive me for my narrow, self-serving attitude. I asked Him to somehow, in some way, change me so I could serve better. After all, my stated purpose is to inspire OTHERS to greatness. Not myself. OTHERS.

My Personal Challenge to Myself (and maybe you?)

- In business – whatever your business is – focus completely on OTHERS. Completely.
- In relationships – quit the narrow thought process of "what can I get?" Be a true giver with your heart and soul.
- In interactions with family and friends – seek their good and their interests, not just yours.

I never want to pretend to anyone that I am a great leader or a great man. I want to strive towards greatness by putting others first. It is a lifelong quest!

My mentor gave me a little sign before he passed away. It sits on my desk and it reads "Others." And it's just that simple.

How Are You Keeping Score

"I got a sinking feeling in my mid-section ..."

Robert Roberts writes about a fourth grade class in which the teacher introduces the "Balloon Stomp." A balloon is tied to every child's leg. The signal is given, and then the object of the game is to pop everyone else's balloon while protecting your own.

Balloon stomp is a zero-sum game. If I win, you lose. Everyone else's success diminishes mine. I must regard others as someone to overcome. Survival of the fittest! Eat or be eaten!

It was a balloon brawl. Some of the shyer students tried in vain to hide on the edges only to be popped! The battle lasted only seconds. And when the final student stood proudly with their balloon intact, no one cheered. There was complete silence. He was the most secretly disliked kid in the room.

Then a worrisome thing happened. A second class emerged to play the game. A class of developmentally challenged children. They were given balloons and the same instructions. "I got a sinking feeling in my mid-section," said one of the onlookers. How can we spare these kids from the balloon brawl?

Only this time, as the instructions were given in haste, the students only grasped that the balloons were to be popped. So, instead of fighting, they helped each other. They formed a kind of "balloon stomp co-op." They held each other's balloons, and they assisted each other in sitting on them until they popped.

Every time they heard a pop, they all cheered and smiled and clapped their hands. And when the final balloon popped, they cheered louder and hugged each other and passed around high fives. There were big smiles!

It was a representation of a scoring system that was a little different. The second class did not score against one another, but with each other. They were no longer opponents, but teammates! It was a win-win situation!

How Do Leaders Keep Score?

1. Look to "team up" with like-minded win-win people. Your success will be compounded.

2. Go out of your way to acknowledge and celebrate others' successes. You'll build bridges and goodwill!

3. Remove envy from the heart. It is insidious and only causes you to play small.

4. Be more joyful and carefree. Be less uptight and competitive. Life is short!

5. The best way to keep score is if we can win together! It cultivates powerful emotions and energy.

The Hot Seat

I've been a part of dozens of corporate and business events and retreats. After a while they kind of blur together. It is the same hotel conference room. The same curiously similar buffet table. Always the ridiculously poor lighting at the podium. But the people are what make it special.

Recently, I was presenting at a corporate leadership retreat on Emotional Intelligence for Extraordinary Leadership. It was a really great morning of dynamic interaction. The CEO of the organization was truly exceptional; he had stunning leadership execution. But honestly, he captivates you with his people skills, his smile, his wit, and his unique ability to involve each person. You feel yourself elevating in thought and conversation just by being in his presence. Plus, he had a contagious laugh that you just couldn't get enough of.

The Defining Moment of the Retreat

On the second day of our retreat (the CEO actually called them "Advances" because his company never retreats), the CEO came up to the front to address everyone in the room. The previous morning, I had described an example of a company where they take time each month to place a team member in the "Hot Seat." When the team member is sitting in the Hot Seat, everyone goes around the room and talks about how that person contributes, shines, makes a difference, and works hard to put skin on their goals as a company. It is a truly special moment for everyone.

Sometimes when I share that story I can almost feel people rolling their eyes. Sometimes I even see them do it. Tough-minded types don't like warm-and-fuzzy moments. Business and leadership is not for the faint of heart. It is a jungle out there and if you can't step up and perform, then you will find yourself in the junkyard!

So here was this CEO, in front of his team. He stood and addressed the room, stating that he would like to do the Hot Seat activity – but with a little twist. Then he walked around the room, stopping at each person. He literally placed his hand on each team member's shoulder and talked about the stunning success contributions that each person had made. I kept thinking, "Where are his cheat sheets?" But he didn't have any. I watched in wonder as the faces of each person lit up at his words. Each person looked newly inspired. I was witnessing the power of communicating personal value. Just those two or three minutes of recognition healed, emboldened, and filled hearts with a renewed courage to continue on!

What a leader. What a magical moment.

And Then The Surprise!

If that moment wasn't enough, he turned to me. Yes, little ol' me in the corner taking it all in. He actually said – and I won't forget the words – "And now, I left the best for the end – Steve Gutzler."

As he walked toward me, my heart started pounding. My eyes moistened. When he placed his hand on my shoulder and spoke glowingly, I melted. I faked a cool demeanor and a soft smile. But inside, I was a puddle. I have those words recorded in my mind. I return to them often because in my world, as I am sure it is in yours, I have many small voices. Sometimes even my own voice is speaking small to me.

But on that day, I found myself striving to live up to those words of greatness. Emotional Intelligence can mean a lot of things to a lot of people. For me, it is something you experience and I attempt to deliver to one person at a time. One conversation, one smile, one handshake, one leadership moment at a time.

"Inspiring others begins with loving others and believing in them."

– Steve Gutzler

Questions to Build Momentum in: Appreciation

1. Who do you need to appreciate? List the top five people who come to mind and commit to verbally appreciating them.

_____

_____

_____

_____

2. In what ways do you give back to your community at a local or global level? How could you contribute more fully as an expression of appreciation?

_____

_____

_____

_____

3. Are there any areas of your life where competition is paramount? Can you make those situations win-win?

_____

_____

_____

_____

Thoughts Around Appreciation

I found seven words make a world of difference in someone's life ... "Thank you. I appreciate what you do." – Steve Gutzler

As we express our gratitude, we must never forget that the highest appreciation is not to utter words, but to live by them. – John F. Kennedy

Make it a habit to tell people thank you. To express your appreciation, sincerely and without the expectation of anything in return. Be a giver – life will be more enjoyable. – Tom and Carolyn Gutzler

To be more childlike, you don't have to give up being an adult. The fully integrated person is capable of being both an adult and a child simultaneously. Recapture the childlike feelings of wide-eyed excitement, spontaneous appreciation, cutting loose, and being full of awe and wonder at this magnificent universe. – Wayne Dyer

Gratitude makes sense of our past, brings peace for today, and creates a vision for tomorrow. – Melody Beattie

Gratitude can transform common days into thanksgivings, turn routine days into joy, and change ordinary opportunities into blessings. – William Arthur Ward

Chapter 10: Celebration

"Encourage 'smart failures' and grant permission to stretch limits." - Steve Gutzler

Come On, Let's Dance!

"Come on, Steve, let's dance! Please, let's dance!"

When Julie and I were first dating and then early into our married life, we loved to dance. Now, I'm not that great a dancer – but I think I am! I grew up with *Saturday Night Fever* and John Travolta, and I actually convinced myself I was on par with his sexy moves and unstoppable poses.

Julie and I never mastered choreographed moves like you see now on "Dancing with the Stars." We were more "shake your body" with no rhyme, no reason, no real method to the madness. I always knew it was a good night if Julie finally whispered in my ear, "You look like an idiot." Or if we were dripping with sweat and all the rest of the dancers had moved several yards away.

But over time, life happened – kids came, bills mounted, schedules filled with soccer and football and baseball, there were sleepovers, mortgage payments, petty disagreements, and serious work. No more dancing for "Serious Steve." Saturday Night Fever became Saturday Night Recovery. Then one day, out of the blue, after a football tournament for my son, we were with a group of parents and heard music off in the distance from a night club. It was Saturday Night Fever type of music ...

Julie looked at me and said, "Come on, Steve. Let's dance!" We proceeded to lead the whole over-the-hill gang into the bar and danced to our little hearts' desires until dawn. Well, not exactly dawn, but at least close to 1 a.m.! I hadn't seen that type of night since my Travolta days!

This next part is completely true. Julie and I now dance at least once a month. That is a lot for us. Sometimes we will go out with friends or follow our favorite Seattle band, the BGP. We dance and we laugh and Julie still tells me that I look like an idiot, now more than once a night.

Leadership Application

Can you roll out a little fun this year? Can you say, "Come on, let's dance!"

It is vitally important to maintain your energy and prevent burnouts. One of the most effective ways to do so is to plan fun and relaxation into your schedule. This is time that you deliberately put aside for unwinding and rebuilding. Dancing is a great example because it is fun, it is silly, and it is good exercise. Do something you enjoy that gets your heart pumping, your laugh booming, and your body moving. You'll be a stronger, more sustainable leader when you do.

Try this: Set some time on your calendar for a "date night" and go dancing! Join the "you look like an idiot" club.

Try this: Set some ridiculously fantastic and stunning new goals that make you smile and dance.

Try this: Don't worry so much about what you look like on the dance floor and get out there. Do it in your business, too! Shake that business booty a little. Shake it up and try some new things!

Try this: Don't be so serious. Some of the most extraordinary and successful leaders I know are a blast to be around. And they can dance – or at least they think they can!

Try this: Recreational, or *"re-create-tional,"* activities put a smile on your face and a skip in your step. Why not take up some dancing lessons? Come on, let's dance!

Try this: Just go dancing!

Leadership Note:

I know most of us have families and careers and real-life pressures. We have goals and aspirations, our own desires for excellence and personal growth. We have financial responsibilities and worries. This is my simple, heartfelt attempt to remind my readers and myself that sometimes we need to just break out and dance.

"Don't leave magical moments to chance – create them!" – Steve Gutzler

Questions to Build Momentum in: Celebration

1.   What are your top three "fun-factor" activities?

_____

_____

_____

2.   Which of the above activities can you engage in within the next week?

_____

_____

_____

3.   What is one recent win you could take a moment to celebrate?

_____

_____

_____

Thoughts Around Celebration

Celebrate what's good about your life. Celebrate a private victory, a day well lived. – Steve Gutzler

Whatever is true, whatever is noble, whatever is right, whatever is pure, whatever is lovely, whatever is admirable – if anything is excellent or praiseworthy – think about such things. – Paul the Apostle

The more you praise and celebrate your life, the more there is in life to celebrate. – Oprah Winfrey

Celebrate your successes and find some humor in your failures. – Sam Walton

I believe if you keep the faith, you keep your trust, you keep the right attitude, if you're grateful and celebrate small things, you'll see God open new doors. – Joel Osteen

When I was working on the movie Lone Survivor, all I cared about was it was done right to honor all of the guys. – Marcus Luttrell, Navy SEAL

Nothing limits achievement like small thinking; nothing expands possibilities like unleashed thinking. – William Arthur Ward

I've found the more I celebrate, the more there is to celebrate. I attract what I project. – Steve Gutzler

Conclusion

"Joy and your splash happen on the way to fulfillment." – Steve Gutzler

Dr. Martin Seligman, past president of the American Psychological Association, believes there are five factors that contribute substantially to our happiness: positive emotion and pleasure, achievement, relationships, engagement and meaning. Of these, he believes engagement and meaning are the most important. Becoming more engaged in what we do by finding ways to make our life more meaningful is the surest way to find lasting happiness ... our *splash*!

When our daily actions fulfill a bigger purpose, the most enduring joy and happiness can happen.

Before he passed away from leukemia, my spiritual mentor, Ron Mehl, gave me a small sign he kept next to his desk in his office. It has one word: "others." I keep that in my office now as a daily reminder of my deeper meaning and splash, which is found by "inspiring greatness in others."

I hope each of the 10 traits have fueled and inspired you and provided the momentum you need to reach for a bigger splash and enduring joy. Your hopes and dreams are not too big. Even broken dreams can be rebuilt, and broken hearts healed.

One of the common myths in our culture is that successful people don't have problems or pain. We think marriages magically thrive without struggles or deep challenges, or that some leaders rise to the top simply on the basis of their charisma and smarts. Most everyone I've met or coached has their own set of prescribed challenges, but in the midst of that they have:

1. Found a calling greater than themselves
2. Identified a Code of Honor, eight to 10 promises they make and keep for themselves
3. Discovered a vision, a picture of their future which creates passion in the present
4. Displayed courage to soar with their one-and-only life
5. Secured determined visualization, an ability to push through quitting points
6. Practice resiliency, the ability to turn bad times into good times
7. Rejuvenate with a fresh start; they allow for restoration and renewal
8. Brevity; they choose to invest in what matters most, and most of the time it's people
9. Appreciation; they strive to be less uptight and competitive because life is short
10. Celebration; learning to dance again and fall back in love with life and those they love

Life is too short to pile up a platform of woulda, coulda, shouldas.

Most every morning I'm home, I go on my morning walk with our golden retriever and Doberman. Talk about living a splash with no regrets! Those fun-loving dogs romp, play, and run to their hearts' content on the wooded trails near our home. Come rain or shine, we are out there. It's also my sanctuary, my thinking time. I'm not distracted by technology – it's just two dogs, one man, and a trail. It's there I recount victories and shortcomings. I try to get crystal clear on what I am supposed to accomplish, big and small, with no regrets and no reserve.

Reading Bronnie Ware's 2012 book, *The Top Five Regrets of the Dying*, shook loose so many regrets and reserves I was holding. Ware spent many years caring for those facing their own mortality. When she questioned the dying about any regrets, anything they hadn't done or anything they would do differently, Ware found that common themes surfaced again and again.

In descending order, the five most common were these:

5.   "I wish I had let myself be happier." Too late in life they realized happiness is a choice.

4.   "I wish I'd stayed in touch with my friends." Too often they failed to give their relationships the time and effort they deserved.

3.   "I wish I had the courage to express my feelings." Too frequently they shut their mouths and contained feelings weighing too heavy to handle.

2.   "I wish I hadn't worked so hard." They spent too much time making a living over building a splash and it caused too much remorse.

1.   "I wish I had the courage to live a life true to myself, not the life others expected of me." Their last days were filled with half-realized dreams and unfulfilled hopes. **This was the number one regret expressed by the dying.**

As Ware put it, "Most people had not honored even half of their dreams and had to die knowing that it was due to choices they had made, or not made."

Honoring our own unique *splash* and pursuing our hopes and dreams in fearless faith is a high calling. It is a call to live with no regrets, a call creating momentum in life and leadership.

So, make sure every day you are doing what matters most to you, pursuing work that matters, and engaging in relationships that matter most.

Don't accept your life, lead it!

Making Your *Splash* is an Inside Job

How do you begin living your *splash* every day? With great purpose and solid priorities, with attention to detail to your soul, your heart, and your conscience. Learn to say "yes" to the best. Don't be afraid to say "no" to anything that is less than your best *splash,* one filled with unprecedented success and significance, a life lived for others.

May you begin to feel the power of a life well lived – one splash at a time!

A Splash! Code of Honor

As you think about how to start making a splash in your own life, I wanted to provide you with my own personal Code of Honor. In Chapter 2, we walked through what a code of honor can really mean to you and your efforts to start making a splash in every area of your life. For me, what a code of honor really means is that you can make and keep promises to yourself which then allows you to make and keep promises to those in your life that matter most. I hope that by sharing my personal code you'll be inspired to start making and keeping these promises yourself!

Attitude is First!
• Be positive. Be optimistic.

• Be resilient.

• Have courage and be bold.

Dream Big. Do it!

• Aim high.

• Focus on accomplishments.

• Believe in my gifts.

• Try new things.

Go For The Golden Rule!

• Ask, "What can I do for you?"

• Make character decisions.

• Possess an "others first" mindset.

Walk in Faith!

• Let my life be my message.

• Put faith in the center.

- Love God. Love people.

Learn. Try. Care.

- Read daily.
- Always try and never give up.
- Care about others.

Family Legacy!

- Put family first.
- Model service, gratitude, humility.
- Believe in their purpose.
- Create memories with each moment.

Be a Leader!

- Be a positive influence.
- Impact the world for good.
- Inspire greatness in others.

Be a Corporate Athlete!

- Train 4 – 5 days per week.
- Eat to win.
- Daily supplements.
- Healthy mind - diet.

Have Fun!

- Live life to the fullest!
- Make others laugh.
- Finish strong.

The Journey to Your Splash

If you've gotten to this point in the book, you've likely already got a pretty good idea of the things you want to start doing to make a splash in many different areas of your life. I hope you're excited about making your own splash – I know I'm certainly excited for you! And I know from walking alongside so many of my clients over the years that if you take what you've read and start applying it, your life most certainly will change for the better. Thank you for going on this journey with me!

I've included a few more tools and examples in the last part of this book to help you start outlining how you'll make your splash. If you'd like more information, please visit my website at stevegutzler.com and connect with me on social media. I'd love to hear from you!

Most importantly, I want to encourage you to stay true in your pursuit of your splash. Stay true to what matters most to you. Stay true to who you believe you're called to be. Know that your days truly are filled with unlimited potential that's waiting for you to realize it. Get out there and make your splash!

Splash! Self-Realization Drill

If you want to create a heart-pumping, vital vision for your life, the first step is to take some quality time to reflect on where you have traveled and what has been important to you thus far.

The purpose of the *Self-Realization Drill* is to take stock, to listen, and to learn. Take the time to look within yourself, and remember we are both here to support, encourage, and empower your vision!

The *Self-Realization Drill* is designed to ask the "key questions" that will help you lay a strong foundation for your future vision.

Self-realization is a great tool to help cultivate the soil of your soul, to identify lasting values and dreams, and to create greater vision and clarity.

As you work through the various questions and coaching materials contained in this program, I highly recommend that you document your journey, answers, and thoughts. You might find it useful to make copies of these modules and write your answers directly on the outlines provided. Some find it helpful to record their thoughts in a personal journal or notebook, while others prefer an electronic method, such as a laptop, iPad, and using one of my favorite tools, Evernote note-taking software.

- Set aside regular time to review these questions and share with a trusted colleague, coach, or friend.
- Find a quiet place that is private
- Be deliberate – "open your heart and let the answers spill out on the pages of your story."
- Share your journey with someone you trust
- Be honest, be patient, and have faith

Remember, this is your journey and by recording your thoughts, you are creating a living document that you will breathe life into as you continue to grow and change.

LOOKING BACK ... HIGHS AND LOWS

Describe in one page your life so far in terms of family, career, health, finances, and other key areas of your life.

- Bullet point one "high" and one "low" for each area
- Describe three defining moments that have influenced and shaped your life
- What was "in the box" during the first half of your life? (The box representing those things most important to you: Getting married, purchasing a home, securing a career, having kids, etc.)
- How have these "highs" and "lows" shaped you so far?

QUESTIONS

1. Where have you looked for inspiration, mentors, and working models for your life?

2. Looking back, how did you define success? How would you define success? Does success look different now?

3. What have you most enjoyed and in what areas have you most excelled as you look back on your life to this point?

4. Do you feel you had a clear vision for your personal and professional life? Did you reach that vision?

LOOKING AROUND – WHAT'S IMPORTANT?

1. Are you missing anything in your life in any area right now?

2. What do you value? What are your top 5 values? Do you feel like you have lived your values?

3. Is there something about your current situation that makes you feel fulfilled or makes you feel trapped?

LOOKING AHEAD – WHERE I WANT TO GO!

1. Coaching tip: When you look ahead at the life you want to create, don't get fixated on perfection and instead focus on direction. You can and will perfect your vision of the future as you go.

2. What would you like to be doing five to ten years from now?

3. What do you want to be remembered for? Accomplishments, achievements, personal fulfillments, etc.

4. What about money – how much is enough? If I have more than enough, toward what purpose will I apply the excess?

5. Going forward, what is your passionate ambition?

6. What are the things you enjoy doing most and would like to focus on in the future?

7. Can you describe areas that could provide greater balance, passion, meaning, and joy in your life?

8. What are the important elements of your life that deserve more time?

9. What brings you inner satisfaction and a sense of fulfillment?

10. Write a one-page description of what you would like to accomplish in the next 24 months. (Your inspiration)

Setting Splash! Inspired Goals

You have already accomplished some significant work toward creating your preferred future, your life vision. You've laid a thoughtful, authentic foundation – which is crucial. You've identified and crafted your purpose and documented the cornerstone values which will help to ensure your success. You have also taken the time to dream. Heart-pumping dreams give you a greater sense of purpose that both pull you forward into tomorrow and enable you to live more fully in the moment today. You've begun creating and detailing your vision of the future you want to live. Now, we are going to shift our focus to transforming your dreams and priorities into realities.

While dreams are about your vision of the future, goals are about the actions you will take today. Goal setting is a powerful process for thinking about your ideal future and then determining what specific actions are required to make that vision real. By becoming more aware of precisely what you want, you more quickly recognize distractions, get yourself back on course, and begin to focus your energies and efforts on the most meaningful action. The process of goal setting helps you make choices that will take you where you really want to go and achieve what you really want to accomplish.

One of my goals is to inspire you to learn the powerful art of goal setting. Writing specific goals around your *"Seven Key Areas"* in life – Family & Relationships, Career, Health & Fitness, Finances, Personal Development, Fun Factor, and Spiritual Peace – can be incredibly motivating. And, over time, as you get in the habit of setting and then achieving your goals, you will find that your self-confidence, self-esteem, and personal sense of power soar.

ACHIEVEMENT – SUCCESS – FOCUS

"Failure isn't 'not reaching your goals.' Failure is 'not setting your goals and then striving until you achieve them.'"

Top business professionals, world-class athletes, and most high-performance individuals all utilize some form of goal-setting technique. Goal setting arms you with the double-edged sword of long-term vision and short-term motivation. Goals focus your mind and help you organize each day around actions that will bring your dreams to life in the real world. By setting crystal-clear, sharp, specific goals, you can measure your progress and take pride in realizing your dreams.

GOAL SETTING AROUND THE SEVEN KEY AREAS

Your first step in learning to set goals will be to consider what you want to achieve in your lifetime and then, more specifically, what you want to achieve in the next five years that will move you meaningfully toward those lifelong goals. Once you gain confidence and experience, you can build your plan out to 10 years and then further.

To provide your goal-setting process with balance, we suggest setting three specific goals – a *five-year goal*, a *one-year goal*, and a *60-day goal* in each of the "Seven Key Areas" of your life. We have also provided you with some powerful, inward-looking questions to help stimulate your thinking as you formulate your goals. The answers to these questions may form the core of some of the goals you set for yourself.

1. FAMILY & RELATIONSHIPS
    - How can you turn a good marriage into a great one?
    - What values are you striving to model to your children?

EXAMPLES

- 5-YEAR GOAL: Set up a college fund for each of my five children which provides for half of their education and then build it over the next five years.
- 1-YEAR GOAL: Plan and enjoy a Dream-Building Weekend with my wife in the month of May.
- 60-DAY GOAL: Set up one "quality time" activity with each of my children. Get these activities on the calendar in the next 60 days.

2. CAREER
- What level or position do you want to reach in your career?
- Is there an additional new business you would like to start?
- How can you move into the top 10 percent of your field?

EXAMPLES

- 5-YEAR GOAL: Devote my full-time efforts to my new consulting business.
- 1-YEAR GOAL: Create $25,000 revenue in additional business for the coming year.
- 60-DAY GOAL: Set up 12 face-to-face contact meetings and meet with my web designer.

3. HEALTH & FITNESS
- What nutritional guidelines do you want to follow?
- What fitness and exercise priorities have you set?

- What health habits would you like to achieve?

EXAMPLES

- 5-YEAR GOAL: Continue to achieve my ideal weight with exercise four times a week.
- 1-YEAR GOAL: Reach my ideal weight by June of next year.
- 60-DAY GOAL: Purchase and use a new supplement program and go to bed and rise at the same time six days a week.

4. FINANCIAL

- How much do you want to earn annually, this year and at each stage of your career?
- What percentage of your income will be devoted to investment and to savings?
- What percentage of your income will be given to charity or to church?

EXAMPLES

- 5-YEAR GOAL: Purchase one investment property and clear all outstanding debt.
- 1-YEAR GOAL: Meet with a financial planner to recalibrate my financial plan, including investments, savings, college accounts, and charitable giving.
- 60 DAY GOAL: Meet with my spouse to create a workable budget to serve our dreams and motivate our needs.

5. PERSONAL DEVELOPMENT

- Is there any knowledge you want to acquire in particular?
- What information and skills will you need to achieve other goals?

EXAMPLES

- 5-YEAR GOAL: Acquire my master's degree in international business.
- 1-YEAR GOAL: Attend leadership vision summit in May to inspire my dreams.
- 60-DAY GOAL: Read a book around consulting in international business.

6. <u>FUN FACTOR</u>
   - How do you want to enjoy yourself?
   - What fun activities or recreational pursuits fuel the fun factor in your life?
   - What activities put a smile on your face and feed your soul?

EXAMPLES

- 5-YEAR GOAL: Purchase a small house on the lake east of the mountains.
- 1-YEAR GOAL: Purchase some football season tickets and schedule dance lessons.
- 60-DAY GOAL: Sell my boat on Craigslist so we can upgrade next year. Take daily walks with my wife and our dog.

7. <u>SPIRITUAL PEACE</u>
   - What spiritual discipline would you like to start or maintain?
   - What spiritual nourishment and worship times would you like to enjoy?
   - Do you have a spiritual mentor or pastor that leads you and feeds you?

EXAMPLES

- 5-YEAR GOAL: Provide practical leadership and examples to each of my children and wife by continuing to attend worship services.
- 1-YEAR GOAL: Complete my weekly spiritual reading plan by July.
- 60-DAY GOAL: Practice solitude, prayer, and journal my highs and lows at least three mornings a week.

GOAL SETTING TIPS

VERBALIZE YOUR GOALS:

Once you've set your goals, be sure to state them aloud. As you speak them, your goals will become a part of your internal drive system. As your mind thinks about your goals, your will to achieve them will increase.

BE CRYSTAL CLEAR:

Set a precise goal, putting in dates, times, and amounts so that you measure achievement. If you do this, you will know exactly when you have achieved the goal, and can take complete satisfaction from having achieved it.

LOCK DOWN YOUR PRIORITIES:

When you have several goals, give each a priority. This helps you to avoid feeling overwhelmed by too many goals, and helps to direct your attention to the most important ones.

WRITE GOALS DOWN:

Writing your goals down crystallizes them and gives them more focus. You can keep your goals on a 3"x5" card on your computer or any place that will ensure that you see them on a frequent basis.

KEEP GOALS SMALL:

Keep the specific goal you are working toward small and achievable. If a goal is too large, it can seem that you are not progressing toward it. Keeping goals small and incremental provides more opportunities for success and reward.

SET PERFORMANCE GOALS, NOT OUTCOME GOALS:

Set goals over which you have as much control as possible. Nothing is more dispiriting than failing to achieve a goal for reasons beyond your control. In business, these could be a poor business climate or the unexpected effects of government policy. In sports, these could include poor officiating, inclement weather, or injury. Goals based on performance keep you in control of their achievement and give you a sense of satisfaction when they are achieved.

SET REALISTIC GOALS:

Set goals you can achieve. Be aware that employers, parents, the media, and society at large can fill our mind with unrealistic self-expectations. We, too, can set unrealistic goals for ourselves if we do not appreciate the obstacles.

Now, connect with me on social media and tell me how your goals are progressing!

Acknowledgements

The writing of Splash, like most of the things in my life, is an act of teamwork. I'd like to sincerely thank the people who helped me visualize this book and then create it.

- Julie Gutzler, my wife, best friend, and model of love and splashing fun times!
- The Leadership Quest team who helped me think through Splash and the Ten Remarkable Traits to Build Momentum in Life and Leadership.
- Brittany Flajole (Blondino) who did a wonderful job of helping in formatting themes and typing our first draft.
- Jamie Filotei, my trusted Executive Assistant, who managed our process and kept me on track. You always take care of the details that allow me to be at my best. My former assistant, Alyssa Turner, was also critical in helping the early drafts of Splash! take shape.
- Ivy Sprague, who sharpened the manuscript by proofreading and editing with excellence.
- My three loving children, their two spouses, and our six grandchildren – you generate the Splash inside me that creates ripples each day!

Biography

Steve Gutzler is the president of Leadership Quest, a Seattle-based leadership development company. Steve is a dynamic, highly sought-after speaker who has delivered more than 2,500 presentations to a list of clients including Microsoft, Starbucks, the Seattle Seahawks, Pandora Radio, Boeing, Cisco, Starwood Corporation, the Ritz Carlton group, and the U.S. Social Security Administration – to name just a few.

Leadership Matters

Steve's exceptional ability to communicate clear leadership and business/sales solutions with humor, clarity and insight is why he is in such high demand. Steve believes every presentation should transform a life and inspire leadership. He presents with passion and conviction to groups of 50 to more than 5,000 intimately in his high-performance "Emotional Intelligence for Leadership" and "Unleash the Leader Inside of You" programs. He knows how to deliver proven results and has been engaging and inspiring audiences with his messages of extraordinary leadership, achievement, success, and significance for more than 25 years.

Experience Matters

Having coached and trained CEOs, presidents, professional athletes, and world-class organizations, Steve's insights have earned him a reputation around the world as an authority on high performance leadership, emotional intelligence for exceptional leadership, growing leaders at every level and accelerating sales success.

Steve is a regular guest on T.V. and radio. He recently was voted #1 by the readership of Huffington Post as the Most Inspirational Leader on Social Media.

A published author on leadership and Emotional Intelligence, Steve is widely read and enjoys interacting with his thousands of Twitter followers. He resides near Seattle with his wife Julie where they enjoy time with their three adult children and six grandchildren.

Made in the USA
San Bernardino, CA
06 January 2018